Using the Strategy Process Cycle to Develop Competitive Advantage

George H. (Jody) Tompson, PhD

Photo by Jackman Chiu on www.unsplash.com

Preface

The field of strategic management is focused on answering questions about organizational performance. In other words, we want to uncover the reasons for why some organizations are so much more successful than others. When people learn that I teach courses in strategic management, they often have questions. The two most common questions are something like the following.

- "What strategies are the best companies using these days?"
- "It seems like strategy is mostly just common sense….how can you teach a strategy?"

Those questions assume there is a "best strategy" that can be discovered and then explained. As if any manager could decipher the strategy of Amazon, Tesla, or Apple and adopt it into his or her company. In a roundabout way, the purpose of this book is to show that those questions are not the best ones to ask. Instead of promoting a particular strategy or claiming that there is a "best" strategy, this book explains how to think about strategy, not so much what strategy to pick. "How to think" points to a process. There is a process for learning to ride a bike, play a piano, or speak a new language. Good strategy occurs when a management team has a good process for designing strategy. A good process will help create a favorable outcome. This book presents the "Strategy Process Cycle" as one method for creating effective strategy. It's not the only method for how to think about strategy, but it is concise, powerful, and should help managers draw astute insights into the situations that any organization is facing. I hope you find it useful and I hope after you have studied it you will have begun to develop your own process for thinking strategically – happy strategizing

Preface to the 3rd Edition

For this edition of <u>How Strategy Works</u>, every chapter was evaluated and (hopefully improved). During the four years since the last edition, I made regular notes for how and why to upgrade the book. In total, about 4000 words and 15 pages were added to this edition. There are two obvious changes at the beginning and ending of each chapter. First, each chapter begins with an "Opening Vignette" that is a small case study about a familiar company. Each was written with the goal of illustrating a key concept that appears later in the chapter. Each of the companies will be familiar to most students, but concept being illustrated might be less familiar. The "Opening Vignette" for each chapter is completely new in the 3rd edition. The vignettes can be used as the basis for a class discussion or as material to reinforce some of the material in the chapter. Second, a new section was added at the end of each chapter. "For Further Consideration" contains material that didn't quite seem necessary for inclusion in the text, but does add thought-provoking ideas that pertain to the material.

Dedication

Over the years, my understanding of strategy has focused less on analyzing facts about companies and industries, and instead, focused more on leadership. Any strategy can only become successful when excellent leaders are at the helm. I thank my wife Holly Tompson for her contribution to my appreciation for excellent leadership. She has developed an amazing blend of skills as a professor, executive coach, speaker, and leader. My views on "how strategy works" have been shaped by our many years together. Even more impressive than her professional accomplishments, she manages to be an extraordinary spouse, and mother to our children.

Table of Contents

"Descending the western arête of the Pointe des Écrins" by Mahoney, James (1816-1879) Scanned wood engraving appearing in Whymper, Edward (1871) <u>Scrambles amongst the Alps in the years 1860-69</u> London: John Murray Press.

Chapter 1:
Setting Strategic Direction

Chapter 1 addresses how leaders can (and should) dream about an attractive future for their organizations. Setting direction for an organization is a crucial activity for any leader. The best leaders are visionary – they create and promulgate an attractive future that other people can adopt. When describing the components of a company's future, several concepts are important, but many have come to be used interchangeably. For example, the words "strategy," "goal," "mission," and "vision" are critical parts of the strategic management process and they have unique definitions. Unfortunately, they are occasionally used incorrectly. This chapter will help clarify the meanings of these concepts and explain the basic process of strategy that comprises the remainder of the book.

Learning Objectives for Chapter 1:

1. Understand the Five Elements of Strategy
2. Examine some common definitions of strategy
3. Distinguish between an organization's mission and vision
4. Understand the characteristics of strategic decisions
5. Understand the Strategy Process Cycle
6. Distinguish between groups and teams

Opening Vignette for Chapter 1

Do you ever examine the cover of a book you are reading? Usually, an author chooses an image with the intent of conveying a key message. Instead of a random but beautiful image, the author chooses something that contains meaning and represents some of the book's content. The cover on a novel might display an impotent point in the story – something the author believes is memorable or pivotal. A biography will often show an image of the subject so the reader can begin to appreciate the appearance of the focus of the book. In a similar way, a textbook author usually chooses a cover image to express an important message. The image on this page is the cover to the previous version of the book. What message is implied? Sounds like a good essay question on an exam or a class discussion in the first week of the semester: "How is strategy like the game of chess?"

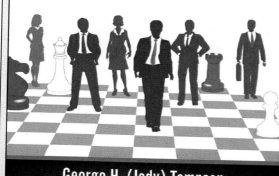

Good chess players think about the present and the future situations <u>at the same time</u>. The <u>present</u> situation is the positioning of the pieces on the board, relative to the opponent's pieces. The <u>future</u> situation must be imagined and then created. A good chess player thinks about the next move, but also plans for several moves in the future, which requires an accurate prediction about the opponent's moves. Another similarity between chess and strategy regards the deployment of personnel. Each chess piece has unique capabilities. A bishop, for example, can only move diagonally. In organizations, good strategy must take into account the capabilities of the employees. For these two reasons (and several others) the game of chess is a pretty good analogy for strategy in an organization, but the analogy has some weaknesses too. Can you think of any? How is chess <u>unlike</u> strategy in organizations? As my appreciation for strategy has evolved over the last three years, I realize a chess analogy emphasizes an ***intellectual*** activity but minimizes the right ***actions*** and ***behaviors*** to make strategy happen. "Choosing a good chess move is intellectually complex but behaviorally trivial: when a decision is made, the player reaches across the board and moves the piece to a new square" (Powell, 2017:166). Chess imitates the intellectual part of strategic management, but has nothing to offer about the behavioral part of strategy. For this third edition, I have chosen a different image for the cover of the book. Here's another good essay question: *"Compared to chess, how is mountain climbing a better representation of strategy in organizations?"*

The Five Elements of Strategy

Sometimes, an idea becomes very popular, but then seems to linger for longer than might be expected. The concept of "strategy" and "strategic" might qualify as management buzz words that have become overused. Ignatova (2017) researched LinkedIn to determine the most common words on recruiter profiles and on company profile pages. The only word to appear on both lists: *strategic*. Almost two decades earlier Hambrick and Frederickson (2001) began noticing that the concept was already being over-used. They contributed to the field of strategy by identifying the five elements that must constitute strategy. The misuse of strategy is illustrated in phrases that they discovered in annual reports and press releases of real companies, such as "Our strategy is to be the low cost provider." What's wrong with that sentence? According to Hambrick & Frederickson, achieving low costs is a good idea but low cost (by itself) is not a fully developed strategy. Another company claimed "Our strategy is to move from defense to industrial applications." The statement sounds promising, but simply identifying a new market is not a strategy (Hambrick & Frederickson, 2001:48). Strategy is an ongoing process, designed with the intent of goal attainment. Implied in this definition is the idea that strategy must be comprehensive – it must reflect all facets of the organization – so that managers do not have blind spots in their view of the company or industry. The five elements of strategy are: arenas, vehicles, differentiators, staging, and economic logic.

Figure 1.1: Is Everything Strategic?

➢ <u>Arenas</u> answers the question "*where* will we compete?" Leaders must realize organizations cannot compete in all geographical markets, all product lines, all stages of the industry production chain, and all customer segments. Instead, strategy must be designed with <u>intentional trade-offs</u> in mind. All organizations have limited resources, and decisions must be made about what activities to pursue, and what activities to decline. As an example, consider the Pharmaceutical Division of Bausch & Lomb, Inc. Managers have identified two main arenas for their strategy: selling pharmaceuticals that treat disease in the "front of the eye" and the "back of the eye." There are different diseases that afflict each segment, different drug treatments and delivery methods, and the two markets have a different revenue size and growth rate.

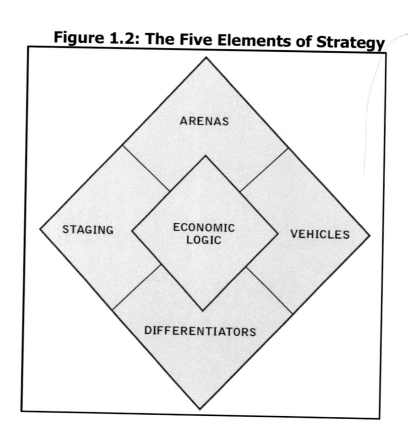

Figure 1.2: The Five Elements of Strategy

ARENAS

STAGING

ECONOMIC LOGIC

VEHICLES

DIFFERENTIATORS

➢ <u>Vehicles</u> answers the question "*how* will we get to the arenas?" In this element, Hambrick and Frederickson recognize that there are many possible ways to arrive at an arena. Good strategists must explicitly describe the vehicle that will be applied. If a company plans to begin competing in a new geographical market (the new arena), managers must then decide whether to use a joint venture, a licensing agreement, an import/export agreement, or maybe establish a wholly-owned distribution facility in the new region. Any of these choices will have advantages and disadvantages that must be identified and evaluated. Identifying an arena (such as a new geographic market) but not a vehicle for travelling to the market would leave a company with an incomplete strategy.

➢ Differentiators describe how the organization will establish uniqueness in the market – uniqueness that will be appealing to customers. Competition is prevalent in all industries (including industries of non-profit organizations) and successful strategy requires differentiation. A common mistake in working with this element of strategy is to assume that differentiators apply only to objective features of the organization's products or service (e.g. "let's offer our product in six colors, because the competitor offers only four colors"). Instead, differentiators can be created in dozens of ways across the organization. For instance, Dell Corporation differentiated itself not on the features of its PCs, but because it was the first in the PC industry to perfect e-commerce and mass customization. The hardware that Dell sold to its customers was not distinctive in the market, but the speed of delivery was unusual (most brands of PCs were already very similar by the mid-1980s). For many people, Nike shoes are their favorite athletic shoe brand not because the shoes are "better" than the others, but because Nike has endorsement contracts with the highest profile professional athletes. Superstar athletes can have a powerful influence over consumers who are deciding which brand of shoe to buy. LeBron James and Cristiano Ronaldo each have a *lifetime* endorsement contract with Nike, purported to be worth about $1 billion. Whatever the benefit a differentiator provides, its ultimate goal is to provide value to customers for which they are willing to pay. Chapter 3 fully explores the notion of differentiation.

➢ Staging – The arenas, vehicles, and differentiators might be called the "content" of an organization's strategy, but they don't describe the speed or the pace for which the content should be implemented. In most strategies, activities must happen at different times or sequences. Some activities must be started before others and some must be completed before others can begin. As a simple analogy, imagine the planning that must be done to build a house. An obvious part of the plan is a detailed schedule that tells the workers what tasks must be completed first, second, third, etc. The foundation must be completed (and inspected) before the workers begin framing up the walls. And the framing must be completed before the roof trusses can be installed. When leaders plan the staging as an element of strategy, the sequence of events might be less obvious. For instance, when a management team wants to expand a company's product into a new country, should marketing research be conducted before negotiating with a distribution company in the new country? Questions about the staging of activities are not always easy to answer. In some cases, incorrect staging can cause a strategy to fail even if the other elements of strategy are impeccable. Many fledgling entrepreneurs spend hundreds of hours writing and revising their business plans. Business plans are important, but it is possible to place too much emphasis on writing the document when instead, the entrepreneur could be out in the marketplace, talking to potential customers and collecting accurate feedback about the new product or service. Reliable data about the product would be much more valuable than spending another week perfecting the business plan.

➤ Economic Logic is the fundamental mechanism by which the company will earn economic viability. Even non-profit organizations must meet economic goals, so their strategies must include a compelling economic logic. In this element of strategy, leaders must have clear and compelling answers to questions like "will economies of scale allow us to have the lowest cost structure in the industry?" or "does our quality allow us to compete with premium pricing?" In a nutshell, a strategy's economic logic explains how the company will earn a profit. Steinway & Sons is a piano manufacturer headquartered in New York City. It is widely regarded as the company that makes the best pianos in the world. Professional pianists often demand that concert halls be equipped with a Steinway. Building a Steinway grand piano takes about a year to complete and contains about 12,000 parts. New Steinway grand pianos start at a retail price of almost $100,000. What is the economic logic of this company's strategy? In spite of increasing threats from digital pianos and keyboards, Steinway is still preferred by the most demanding customers in the world. Professional musicians, concert halls, universities, and wealthy individuals are the target market for Steinway & Sons. Since the company was founded in 1853, this target market has been willing to pay top prices to obtain the world's best piano. Compared to its competitors, Steinway & Sons has high costs of labor, raw materials, and inventory. But it converts those inputs into a product that is unrivaled in the industry. The economic logic of Steinway's strategy has proven to be successful for many years. In my many years of experience at The University of Tampa, economic logic is the element of strategy that is the most difficult one for students to master in their projects with companies. Instinctively, we all know that a good strategy must create benefits for the organization: increase revenue or lower costs (or both). Additionally, those benefits must outweigh the costs. Cost/benefit logic is easy to understand, but usually difficult to demonstrate. Excellent strategic thinking requires a compelling case to be made for how the benefits of a strategy will outweigh its costs. In many situations, a discounted cash flow analysis or an internal rate of return is not convenient or even feasible. A break-even analysis is usually simpler, but even if that calculation is not possible, a strategist must still include some cost/benefit logic in the explanation of a strategy.

By adhering to all five elements of strategy, leaders are more prepared to create strategies that are comprehensive and balanced. According to Hambrick and Frederickson (2001) most companies have a tendency to emphasize one or two elements of strategy, usually at the expense of the other elements. A more effective approach is to build a strategy with all five elements.

Defining Strategy

To consider the definition of strategy begs the question "the strategy of *what?*" Strategy implies some kind of organization, with leaders who are making decisions about how the organization should proceed into the future. Mintzberg noted that "Every organized human activity -- from the making of pots to the placing of a man on the moon -- gives rise to two fundamental and opposing requirements: The division of labor into various tasks to be performed, and the coordination of these tasks to accomplish the activity" (1992). So, in this book, we will be studying how strategy happens in organizations. The word "strategy" is based on the Greek word *stratēgos*, which is a combination of *stratos* (army) and *ago* (leading). While the original concept of strategy had a distinctive military implication of leading an army, authors in business and management began using the term in the 1950s to emphasize a holistic view of managing an entire enterprise. Until that time, there was less recognition of integrating the various functions of an organization. For example, integrating the goals of the marketing department with the goals of the finance department would not have been a common theme in organizations. Instead, the departments were more likely to function as semi-autonomous units. Even today, departments sometimes have trouble communicating and agreeing on decisions (see Chapter 5). The marketing department might not agree with the cost control decisions made by the accounting department. One of the earliest uses of the concept of strategy in a management context was Selznick (1957), who recognized that successful companies were able to align their resources and assets across functional departments, but he also emphasized how organizations should align themselves with the conditions in their industry or market. In other words, the internal environment of the successful company was designed to match the situation that managers discovered in the external environment. The alignment of the external and internal environments formed the basis of the SWOT analysis (strengths, weaknesses, opportunities, threats). Another scholar who is credited with early contributions to strategic management was Chandler (1962). In a longitudinal study of large companies, he recognized that when the external environment changed, successful companies responded by 1) changing their strategy to match the new environment, and then 2) changing their organizational structures so they could more easily implement the new strategy. So Chandler's ideas advanced the concept of "strategic fit" by recognizing that strategy must align with industry conditions, and must also guide managers' thinking as they design the organization's structure.

Over time, many definitions of strategy have emerged. See Figure 1.3 for a summary of three exemplary definitions. Each of the three has distinguishing or unique characteristics. Henderson's definition is probably the most

> **Figure 1.3:**
> **Exemplary definitions of strategy**
>
> ➤ "A deliberate search for a plan of action that will develop a business's competitive advantage, and compound it" (Henderson, 1989: 141).
> ➤ "Strategy is a firm's theory about how to compete successfully" (Barney, 2002: 6).
> ➤ "Strategies are both plans for the future and patterns from the past" (Mintzberg, 1987: 67).
> ➤ "Strategy is about getting more out of a situation than the starting balance of power would suggest. It is the art of creating power" (Freedman, 2013: xii).

conventional of the three. Many people consider strategy to be synonymous with a <u>plan</u> – a method or technique that companies use to accomplish their goals and guide managers' thinking. Barney's definition emphasizes the fact that strategy is always a work in progress. Even the most experienced managers can't be sure that any strategy will be successful. Just as a theory in science is a speculation about the nature of reality, a manager's strategy is a <u>prediction</u> about what actions will make a company successful in the future. A manager can never know how successful a strategy will be until it is put into action. Just as a theory may require revisions when new knowledge is discovered, a strategy may require revisions when managers realize that competitors, government agencies, or customers are different than expected. Do you remember some basics of high school physics? Newton's Law of Universal Gravitation is a law because it is a description of how the natural world behaves. But a theory explains causality – or in other words a theory tries to explain why things happen the way they do. So, a company's strategy is its statement of causality: "if we do these things, we will cause our company to succeed." Mintzberg's definition contributes the idea that strategy is influenced (and constrained) by previous decisions and results. Most students reading this book are pursuing a career in business. Because of the many decisions over the years that have built their competency in business, these students will probably never practice medicine. So their career strategy today is constrained by the pattern of past decisions. Not all options are (easily) available today. There are other reasons why Mintzberg's definition is helpful. Can you think of any? Freedman is a political scientist and professor of war studies. Because of his background, Freedman's definition of strategy emphasizes that gathering power is important for successful strategy in a competitive environment. Power help a strategist tilt the odds in his or her favor, so that the preferred outcome is more likely to eventuate. Sometimes strategy describes how we participate in a zero-sum game, so we must be willing to pursue gains that will create losses for our opponents. In an ideal world, people, companies, and governments would consistently cooperate to achieve their goals. Until our world is ideal, we compete where resources are limited, greed is prevalent, and conflict is common.

A similarity of all four definitions in Figure 1.3 is their part of speech. All four define strategy as a noun. The perspective in this book is that strategy is certainly a noun, but it is wise to also consider how strategy is an *action*. To convey the idea that strategy is an action, this book defines strategic management as *the process of creating interdependent activities that will enable an organization to compete successfully*. Like any process, this process of strategy has a series of steps that can be practiced and improved. This is important for students to remember: strategic thinking is a skill that can be practiced and developed. Strategy doesn't just happen….it is the result of creative but disciplined strategic thinking. It can be learned like any other skill. A model demonstrating the series of steps will be presented near the end of this chapter.

In addition to understanding the definition of strategy, other concepts are important for managers who are charged with "setting strategic direction." A good starting point is to distinguish between the concepts of <u>mission</u> and <u>vision</u>. In many cases, these words have been used interchangeably. For example, a company called Burt's Bees has identified its Mission <u>and</u> Vision as "We make people's lives better every day — naturally" (www.burtsbees.com). Rather than creating a distinctive vision and mission, the company has chosen to write one statement that covers both concepts. Another common mistake in creating a mission and vision is assuming that both are philosophical statements of goals. It's true that both should be inspirational, but the roles of a mission and vision are different. See Table 1.1 for definitions of each concept.

Table 1.1: Definitions of Mission and Vision

Mission	Vision
➢ Describes the <u>purpose</u> of the organization.	➢ The preferred future state (or condition).
➢ Explains "why we work here".	➢ A dream of the 15 year future.
➢ Focus on current business activities.	➢ Focus on future business outcomes.
➢ aka the "Core Ideology" (Collins & Porras, 1996).	➢ aka "Envisioned Future" (Collins & Porras, 1996).

The first row of Table 1.1 provides the most succinct and simple definitions of each concept. Mission is synonymous with the organization's purpose. The mission statement should describe why the organization was created and/or why it exists today. Of course there can be dozens of easy answers to why any organization exists: to create wealth for the owner, to provide jobs for the family or local community, to serve customers, or to build goodwill. However, such "easy" mission statements miss the point of effective strategy and leadership. The reason that mission statements can be effective is that they inspire employees to contribute to a cause greater than themselves. Almost all of us must work to financially support ourselves and our families. But if our concept of work is merely giving labor and then receiving money, then the leaders of our organization have not articulated a clear purpose. In such places, employees can struggle to feel dedicated, especially when work becomes difficult or stressful. Furthermore, there tends to be lower productivity and higher turnover in companies where employees feel disconnected from their purpose. See Figure 1.4 for the mission statement of the Coca-Cola Company.

In a famous illustration, Drucker (1946) recounted the story of a US rifle manufacturing plant during World War II. Because of the shortage of working age men, this factory was staffed by women. They had low job skills and very little knowledge of rifles. As could be expected, the quality and consistency of the rifles was often poor. When the women were given intense job training, they improved the performance of their tasks only marginally. Drucker's solution was to take the women to a firing range along with rifles they had created in the factory. Each woman was shown how her labor contributed to the whole function of the rifle. Maybe her job was merely to insert a screw into the barrel of the gun, but by seeing a completed rifle, holding it in her hands, and learning how to shoot it, she saw a greater purpose in her role on the factory floor. From that point forward, she was still inserting a screw into the barrel of a gun, but she knew that her role was critical for the performance of the rifle, which was critical for the American soldiers fighting overseas. Drucker realized that the low quality rifles were not caused by low job skills, but by the workers feeling isolated and ignorant about the ultimate purpose of their work.

> **Figure 1.4:**
> **Mission of Coca-Cola Company**
>
> ➤ To Refresh the World...in body, mind, and spirit.
> ➤ To Inspire Moments of Optimism...through our brands and our actions.
> ➤ To Create Value and Make a Difference...everywhere we engage.

"Core ideology" is a phrase coined by Collins and Porras (1996) that is synonymous with a company's mission. They describe it as a "consistent identity....that provides the glue that holds the organization together over time" (1996: 66). It includes the company values that are sacred and non-negotiable. Strategy, tactics, markets, and employees may change over time, but the mission should be stable.

> **Figure 1.5: A Vision for Your Career**
>
> 15 years from now:
> ➤ In what industry will you work?
> ➤ How many people will report to you?
> ➤ In what city will you live?
> ➤ What will be your salary range?
> ➤ What will your job description?

A company's vision is a leader's detailed description of the company at some point in the future. It is not a statement of goals, but rather the vivid description of how the company should be, look, act, or perform in the future. Accomplishing a vision is not really measurable, but should be a beacon drawing the organization toward a successful future. The vision describes the company in a perfect but future scenario. As a personal exercise, a business school student might take some time to create a vision for his or her career. Read the questions in Figure 1.5. If you can provide an answer for each question, you have completed the first step in creating a personal career vision. Leaders of companies should follow a similar method of thinking. They should be able to describe the future of the company, and convey that vision to all employees. Collins & Porras (1996) used the term "envisioned future," and encouraged leaders to create BHAGs (big, hairy, audacious goals) as part of their vision. On May 25, 1961 President Kennedy gave a speech in which he set a BHAG for the USA. He promised that before the end of the decade, NASA should "land a man on the Moon and return him safely to the Earth. No single space project in this period will be more impressive to mankind, or more important for the long-range exploration of space; and none will be so difficult or expensive to accomplish." At the time he made this BHAG (mid-1961), NASA had not even accomplished the goal of sending an astronaut into orbit around the earth! Furthermore, the US had fallen behind the Soviet Union in the space race. For President Kennedy to challenge Congress and NASA to send a man to the moon sounded impossible. Despite constant skeptics, his dream became a reality on July 20, 1969. Apollo 11 astronaut Neil Armstrong stepped off the lunar lander and walked on the surface of the moon. In only eight years, NASA had accomplished a BHAG that many people thought was virtually impossible.

A more modern example was in April 2013 when Eric Schmidt (Chairman of Google, Inc.) claimed that "by the end of the decade, everyone on the planet will be connected to the internet" (Stone, 2013:61). At the time Schmidt made the prediction, only about 40% of the world's population had internet access. Not surprisingly, the remaining 60% is located mostly in developing countries and rural areas. It will be interesting to see whether his prediction is accurate, and how big a role Google plays in attempting to achieve this BHAG.

After reading this section, you might be wondering "A leader could never predict the future, so what's the point in trying to describe a detailed vision?" When leaders don't set a vision for their organization, the result is aimlessness. Employees do not have an understanding of where the organization is heading, and they might wonder if the leadership has any real plans for the future. In their research, Collins & Porras compared pairs of companies from the same industry (e.g. Home Depot and Lowe's). In each pair, one of the two companies had established a clear mission and vision while the other had not. Over the course of many years, the performance of the companies in each pair began to diverge. In all the matched pairs of companies, the visionary company performed better. The main conclusion of the research by Collins & Porras is that mission and vision really matters – companies that have visionary leaders tend to have better long-term performance than companies without visionary leaders.

Goals & Objectives

So far, we have distinguished between strategy, mission, and vision. Goals and objectives are statements that companies use to operationalize their mission and vision. Any mission or vision statement tends to be philosophical and difficult to measure. According to the example in Exhibit 2, the mission of Coca-Cola is "to refresh the world." How do leaders of the company know whether they are on track to accomplish their mission? The mission and vision must be converted to short-term, measurable goals that help leaders manage the company's progress. When setting goals and objectives, the following acronym is useful: SMART.

- <u>S</u>pecific – goals should describe exactly what outcome or behavior is expected
- <u>M</u>easurable – goals should be stated so that results can be measured and tracked over time
- <u>A</u>mbitious – goals should challenge people to excellence
- <u>R</u>ealistic – goals should be feasible, so people have a fair chance of meeting them
- <u>T</u>ime-Bound – goals should be defined by a deadline

Imagine a CEO who realizes her company is struggling to provide good customer service. She might set a goal for the company by saying "We must improve our customer service!" Most employees in the company would understand this request, but it does not meet the criteria of a SMART goal. A better way of stating the same goal (that adheres to the SMART criteria) would be "Within three months, we will reduce the number of customer complaints by 10% per month." In this version of the statement, the goal is clearly specific and measurable. With a little extra care and concern for customers, it is probably attainable. It is defined by a deadline, and it must be relevant because customer service is important for any organization that has customers.

Characteristics of Strategic Decisions

Setting the direction of an organization requires leaders to make a series of strategic decisions. The remainder of this book explains methods for how leaders can think strategically about the decisions they are making. In today's world, the word "strategic" has become a common adjective, used to describe nearly anything that describes the future. Originally, however, a strategic decision had certain characteristics that distinguished it from a tactical decision. These characteristics are the domain of this book. According to Johnson & Scholes (1993), strategic decisions are distinguished by the following features.

1. Strategic decisions address the <u>scope</u> of an organization's activities. By scope, we mean the number of activities that are performed, or the number of markets pursued, or the countries to which a company exports, etc. Scope indicates breadth of service or activity, defined by boundaries. Leaders must choose which activities belong in the company's scope, and which activities do not.

2. Strategic decisions seek to <u>match the activities of the organization to the environment</u> in which it competes. The next chapter of the book describes some techniques for analyzing an industry. These techniques are important because all industries are in a constant state of change – effective companies must learn whether and how to respond to changes in customers, competitors, governments, etc.

3. Strategic decisions seek to <u>match the activities of the organization to the resources</u> that it controls. In a team sport such as football, the coach is responsible for designing game plans that exploit the team's competencies. For instance, if the offensive backfield contains players with weak passing and catching skills but strong running skills, then the coach should design offensive schemes that make the best use of those competencies. In the same way, leaders of companies should create strategy that is based on the best resources and competencies that the company owns.

4. Strategic decisions have major <u>implications for resources</u>. In other words, strategic decisions are costly. They require large investments of time, energy, personnel, and maybe cash. As part of the planning process, decision makers usually create several alternative plans and then choose the "best" one. Each alternative requires a budget to help estimate its feasibility. Related to this idea is the notion that strategic decisions are relatively rare. They are too big and complex to be made quickly or often.

5. Strategic decisions <u>affect tactical decisions</u>. Because they are resource intensive (#4), strategic decisions set off a wave of other decisions. On 2/26/08, Starbucks closed all of its US stores for 3½ hours to focus on employee training. This decision meant that almost 7000 stores would close down while employees were given in-store training and education (www.starbucks.com). This was obviously a strategic decision made by a leadership team that recognized a need for drastic action. Making the decision set off dozens of other decisions by other people in the company, all the way down to the managers of each individual store.

6. Strategic decisions <u>reflect the values and ethics</u> of the people who make them. People make important decisions based on the norms and values that they hold sacred. For instance, many high-tech firms are now offering sabbaticals to employees. Every four years, managers at Silicon Graphics get 6 weeks of paid sabbatical, which is in addition to their normal vacation time. What are the values that underlie the strategic decision to offer sabbaticals? Probably the recognition that the employees are the most important part of any organization. They should be treated respectfully, which means time for personal growth and reflection.

7. Strategic decisions <u>impact the performance</u> of the organization. By now, this characteristic is probably obvious. The cost, breadth, and difficulty of strategic decisions shows that they are intended to change performance, if not the direction, of the whole company.

Figure 1.6: The Strategy Process Cycle

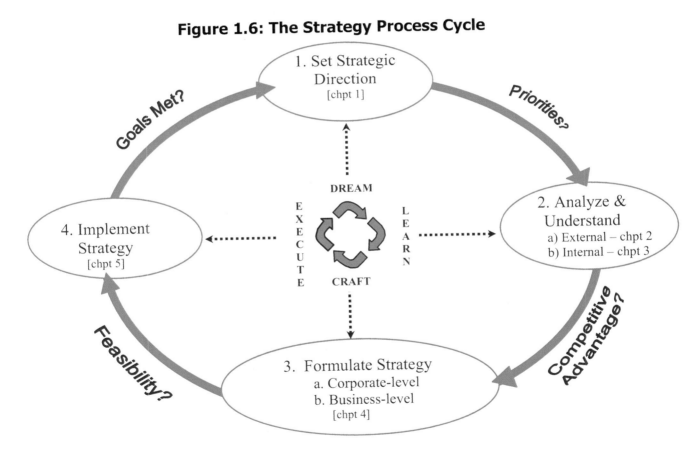

The Strategy Process

At the beginning of this chapter, several definitions of strategy were presented. The question was raised about whether we could consider strategy as an action instead of a noun only. Figure 1.6 shows a model of the strategy process. This model presents strategy as a four step process that makes a cycle. The cycle indicates that strategy is an ongoing action for leaders of an organization.

Step 1 in the process is the subject of this chapter – Setting Strategic Direction. Moving clockwise, the next part of the process is to pass through the first "gate," which is "priorities" in this case. Just like a gate on a fence, the gate only allows passage when it has been opened. After step 1 in the process, leaders must have developed clear priorities for themselves and their organization. Stated differently, the leaders cannot begin analyzing the industry and the organization until they know what is important – until they have established their priorities. The rest of the steps and gates in the model will be covered in the remaining chapters in the book. For now, the following overview will suffice.

The second step is to analyze and understand the environment in which the organization acts. There are two main areas of focus: the external environment (the industry, competitors, etc.) and the internal environment (skills, competencies, and resources controlled by the organization). To pass through the second gate, leaders must have reached an understanding about their organization's competitive advantage. After thorough analysis, leaders should know where their organization is strong and where it is weak. After a comprehensive analysis, the third step is to design or formulate a strategy for the organization. Later in the book, the two levels of strategy will be discussed: corporate-level and business-level strategy. The third gate is the question of feasibility. Most scholars agree that the most difficult part of formulating strategy is making sure that the organization can actually pull it off. Experienced leaders know that they must carefully consider the feasibility of any strategy as a precedent for implementing it. The fourth step is implementing or executing the strategy. This step is widely regarded as the most difficult of the four. Part of implementation should be measuring results to determine if goals are being met. So asking about goal attainment should be the gate leading from implementation back to step 1, or considering the strategic direction of the organization.

The remaining chapters in the book present the other steps in the strategy process. Chapter 2 will address External Analysis (step 2a in the model) and chapter 3 will focus on Internal Analysis (step 2b). Chapter 4 will take up the topic of generic strategies – after a full analysis has been completed, a management team must then identify what strategy to pursue. This chapter will describe the three levels of strategy: corporate, business, and functional strategy. Chapter 5 will address strategy implementation, or how companies execute the strategy that has been articulated in the strategy formulation stage.

As a way to summarize the process, each stage has a one-word motto in the center of the model. Each motto is a verb that captures the main idea of each stage. The mottos appear in the following order: Dream, Learn, Craft, and Execute. To dream is to think about the future of the company, and to set lofty goals for what it will eventually become. To learn implies that there are characteristics of the company and the industry that can be known by the company leaders. One of their jobs is to build an expertise that is better than the expertise of their competitors, which is a function of learning. The third motto is to craft a strategy that will exploit the opportunities available to the organization. Fourth is to execute the strategy that has been crafted.

Strategy and Top Management Teams

Thus far in Chapter 1 we have discussed the definition and the process of strategy, but we have not discussed the origin of strategy. Where does it come from? In a typical organization, strategy is discussed and designed primarily by a team of top managers, usually referred to as the top management team (TMT). According to Wiersema and Bantel (1992: 91) a TMT "identifies environmental opportunities and problems, interprets relevant information, considers organizational capabilities and constraints, and formulates and implements strategic change." In this section, we want to present two features of top management teams that will influence their abilities to create effective strategy. First, let's distinguish between the terms "group" and "team." They are often used interchangeably, but there are some important differences. Table 1.2 summarizes the four different characteristics of teams and groups (Katzenbach & Smith, 1995).

Table 1.2: Groups vs. Teams

Work Teams	Characteristic	Work Groups
➤ Collective performance of the assigned task	1. Main Goal	➤ Individuals perform tasks, then share news
➤ Positive	2. Synergy	➤ Neutral, or sometimes negative
➤ Individual *and* mutual	3. Accountability	➤ Individual
➤ Complementary	4. Skills	➤ Random & varied

1. Main Goal

On a **team**, the main goal is for teammates to work collectively to accomplish a shared task. An obvious analogy is a team sport. When the team plays a game, the outcome is shared by the whole team. The teammates win or lose the game together. Some individuals might perform well while others perform poorly but at the end of the game, one team wins and the other loses. In a work **group**, the goal is to achieve individual outcomes, and then share them with the members of the group. For example, the specific goal of a group might be to gather market information. Each member could be assigned a specific geographic region to study. He or she would do the research, create a report, and then circulate it to the others in the group. The reports might be consolidated into a larger report but each individual retains responsibility for his input.

2. Synergy

A common definition of synergy is when "the whole is greater than the sum of the parts." On a team, there should be encouragement, mutual assistance, and camaraderie so that the teammates are inspired to high performance. A team then will generate greater results than if the individuals were working alone, and then combined their outputs together. A group does not have the same requirements for synergy. Instead of working together, a group is a collection of individuals that has no expectation to inspire each other toward greater teamwork.

3. Accountability

Mutual accountability is probably the most difficult characteristic of teams to master. Individual accountability means that teammates must accept personal responsibility for their contributions to the team effort. They must hold themselves to a high standard. Mutual accountability means that individuals must be accountable to others. Individuals must listen to criticism from the team, they must accept tasks assigned to them, they must agree to the team's goals, and they must admit mistakes when they do not meet the team's standards. Members of a team must allow some vulnerability to their teammates. A teammate must also be willing to gently confront a teammate who is not achieving the team's standards.

4. **Skills**

A team is designed with skills that are complementary. The teammates are assigned to a task with intentionality – the team is created with 1) knowledge of the members' skills and 2) the characteristics of task to be accomplished. Academic research consistently shows that diversity of skills in TMTs helps the teams make higher quality strategic decisions. In contrast, a group is not designed with the same foresight in mind. Each person in a work group must have skills to accomplish his or her task, but there is no expectation that the group will be creating a unified solution or product. Therefore, there is less need to consider how the individual skill sets will complement each other.

The Role of Ethics in Strategic Management

Anyone with even a casual interest in business is well-aware of the recurring stories of ethical failures among business leaders. Many questions are debated about the lapses and failures in business ethics, such as "is white collar crime increasing?" or "why is white collar crime so prevalent?" For a course in strategic management, a more relevant question might be "what are universities doing in response to white collar crime?" According to research by the Association to Advance Collegiate Schools of Business (AACSB), the emphasis on business ethics grew more than any other area of business education from 2008 – 2013 (Davis, 2014). During that five year period, universities increased program offerings in business ethics and corporate social responsibility by about 38%. Comparatively, emphasis on supply chain management grew about 17% while entrepreneurship grew about 13%. Based on these results, business schools believe they can (and should) help students become more ethical leaders.

But how? Can education in a university change the attitudes and behaviors of a person, so that he or she becomes more ethical? Some MBA students at Harvard University believed so. In 2009 they created the "MBA Oath" to encourage business school students to maintain high standards of ethical behavior. See Figure 1.7 to read the MBA Oath. A few themes are noteworthy in the oath. First, the oath acknowledges the importance of teamwork and cooperation. Ethical leaders will refuse the temptation to act unilaterally. Instead, they will work with colleagues, vendors, customers, and local constituents to manage their organizations respectfully and sustainably. This mentality is a shift <u>away</u> from the attitude of "we will follow the law, but we will do whatever we want to earn returns for our shareholders" <u>toward</u> the attitude of "we will respect the desires of other people and organizations to be successful alongside us." Second, the traditional notion of leadership power has been replaced by the idea that <u>an ethical leader must be willing to *serve* other people</u>. Certainly leaders occupy prestigious positions in many organizations, but prestige should not lead to arrogance, entitlement, ruthlessness, or hubris. "Servant leadership" has emerged as a model for leaders who want to lead by the example of being helpful, humble, and honest. In the 1st century, many religious leaders expected a king to emerge as a powerful conqueror in the present day Middle East. He would dominate other kingdoms and overcome the power of the Roman Empire. To the surprise of many, Jesus, the founder of Christianity, arrived as a humble leader who came "not to be served, but to serve" (Matt 20:28). Similarly, the MBA Oath requires leaders to elicit "trust and esteem from those I serve" (last paragraph of MBA Oath).

In recent years, companies in the extraction industries (e.g. mining, oil & gas) have created an approach that illustrates the heart of the MBA Oath. The approach is known as creating a "social license to operate" (SLO) in the communities where the company is located. According to Moffat and Zhang (2014) "For mining companies, it is increasingly evident that obtaining a <u>formal</u> license to operate from governments and meeting regulatory requirements is no longer enough. Instances of mining developments being delayed, interrupted, and even shut down due to public opposition have been extensively documented" (p. 61). The traditional approach to opening a mine, oil well, or manufacturing facility was to acquire governmental approval and licenses to begin construction. Once the licenses were acquired, the company would build and operate the facility with little regard for other stakeholders. Under the SLO approach, companies are seeking involvement from the surrounding communities at the same time they are seeking legal approval from governments. Obtaining both a "social" license and a "legal" license requires companies to consider the negative impacts they might have on the community. When local communities are involved in facility planning from the outset, companies are asked questions about how the new facility will impact the local car & truck traffic, the local schools, the cost of housing, the crime rate, the minimum wage, the tax base, etc. By allowing local stakeholders a voice in the strategic management process, leaders show respect, humility, and authentic interest in sharing success across many constituents. Too many CEOs are viewed as greedy and calloused. On the contrary, the best leaders adopt a leadership style based on humility, service, and collaboration.

Conclusion

Hopefully, you recognized the emphasis that was placed on leadership in chapter 1. Setting the strategic direction for an organization must begin at the top. Excellent leaders know how to solicit ideas from colleagues throughout the organization, but strategy must have its genesis in the planning of the senior management. A leader's job is to create a compelling vision for the organization's future, to promote and clarify the organization's purpose, and to set goals that adhere to the SMART principle. In a sense, leadership serves as the "bookends" for the Strategy Process Cycle. It is fundamental to setting strategic direction in this chapter, and good leadership is also a major topic in Chapter 5 on strategy implementation.

Figure 1.7: The MBA Oath

As a business leader I recognize my role in society.

• My purpose is to lead people and manage resources to create value that no single individual can create alone.

• My decisions affect the well-being of individuals inside and outside my enterprise, today and tomorrow.

Therefore, I promise that:

• I will manage my enterprise with loyalty and care, and will not advance my personal interests at the expense of my enterprise or society.

• I will understand and uphold, in letter and spirit, the laws and contracts governing my conduct and that of my enterprise.

• I will refrain from corruption, unfair competition, or business practices harmful to society.

• I will protect the human rights and dignity of all people affected by my enterprise, and I will oppose discrimination and exploitation.

• I will protect the right of future generations to advance their standard of living and enjoy a healthy planet.

• I will report the performance and risks of my enterprise accurately and honestly.

• I will invest in developing myself and others, helping the management profession continue to advance and create sustainable and inclusive prosperity.

In exercising my professional duties according to these principles, I recognize that my behavior must set an example of integrity, eliciting trust and esteem from those I serve. I will remain accountable to my peers and to society for my actions and for upholding these standards.

Source: www.MBAOath.org

For Further Consideration

Formulating and implementing strategy is known to be a difficult job, even for the most experienced senior managers. Evidence of this view is found in the results of a quarterly survey conducted by the accounting and consulting firm Deloitte, LLP. In the 3rd quarter of 2012 Deloitte asked CFOs about the kinds of decisions that create the biggest struggles for senior managers. See Figure 1.1 for the results of the survey (CFO Journal, 2012). The results indicate that about 60% of executive teams struggle with decisions about creating business strategy. Among all the possible response, business strategy was tied for first place (with organic growth) as the kind of decision that vexes most executive teams.

Figure 1.1: Results from Deloitte, LLP survey in 3rd Quarter 2012

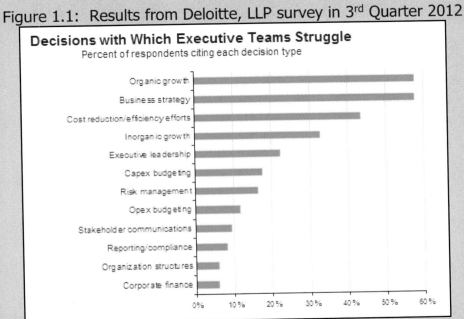

Why is creating a successful strategy so difficult? Before reading the rest of this chapter, consider what you already know about strategy. Maybe you have helped plan the strategy for a school event, or a team sport, or a summer vacation. Use that experience and explain why business strategy seems to be a permanent struggle for companies today.

Questions for Review & Discussion

1. Fill in the blank in each sentence with the correct word to complete a definition of strategy.

a) "Strategy is to company like _____ is to team sport"
b) "A deliberate _____ for a plan of action that will develop a competitive advantage and compound it"
c) "Strategy is a firm's _____ about how to compete successfully"
d) "Strategies are both plans for the future and _____ from the past"

2. Ellis Enterprises, LLC is considering the South American market, specifically targeting Argentina for its custom saddles. This decision involves:
   - A) Arenas
   - B) Vehicles
   - C) Differentiators
   - D) Staging
   - E) Economic Logic

3. Match each of the terms in the left column with their correct definitions in the right column

Term	Definition
1. Arenas	1. Geographic markets in which the company competes.
2. Staging	2. Describes the method that the company will arrive into a market
3. Differentiators	3. The fundamental mechanism by which the company will earn a profit
4. Vehicles	4. The speed or the pace for which strategy should be implemented
5. Economic Logic	5. Describes how the organization will establish uniqueness in the market

4. The terms "team" and "group" are often used interchangeably. According to chapter 1, what are the key differences between the two terms?

5. According to Jay Barney, strategy should be defined as a "theory about how to compete successfully." How is strategy similar to a theory?

6. The Opening Vignette discussed the weakness in using chess as an analogy for strategy. See the answers below for another response to this question.

Answers for Review & Discussion

1.
   a) = game plan
   b) = search
   c) = theory
   d) = patterns

2. The correct answer is A. <u>Arenas</u> answers the question "where will we compete?" <u>Vehicles</u> answers the question "how will we get to the arenas?" <u>Differentiators</u> describe how the organization will establish uniqueness in the marketplace. <u>Staging</u> describes speed of implementation and <u>Economic Logic</u> covers how to earn a profit.

3.
   Arenas = Definition #1
   Staging = Definition #4
   Differentiators = Definition #5
   Vehicles = Definition #2
   Economic Logic = Definition #3

4. Differences between teams and groups

Table 1.2: Groups vs. Teams

Work Teams	Characteristic	Work Groups
➤ Collective performance of the assigned task	1. Main Goal	➤ Individuals perform tasks, then share news
➤ Positive	2. Synergy	➤ Neutral, or sometimes negative
➤ Individual *and* mutual	3. Accountability	➤ Individual
➤ Complementary	4. Skills	➤ Random & varied

5. Barney's definition of strategy emphasizes the fact that strategy is always a work in progress. Even the most experienced managers can't be sure that any strategy will be successful. Just as a theory in science is a speculation about the nature of reality, a manager's strategy is a prediction about what actions will make a company successful in the future. A manager can never know how successful a strategy will be until it is put into action. Just as a theory may require revisions when new knowledge is discovered, a strategy may require revisions when managers realize that competitors, government agencies, or customers are different than expected.

6. "Chess is not a game. Chess is a well-defined form of computation. You may not be able to work out all the answers, but in theory, there must me a solution, a right procedure in any position on the board....Real life strategy consists of bluffing, of little tactics of deception, of asking yourself what is the other man going to think I mean to do." (Poundstone, 1992:6).

References

CFO Journal. (2012). Strategy & growth decisions and major change initiatives add to CFOs' career stresses. Available at http://deloitte.wsj.com/cfo/2012/10/24/

Chandler, A. (1962). Strategy and Structure: Chapters in the history of industrial enterprise. New York: Doubleday.

Collins, J. & Porras, J. (1996). Building your company's vision. Harvard Business Review, Sept-Oct: 65-77.

Davis, E. (2014). Changing Program Composition. Blog of Association to Advance Collegiate Schools of Business. http://aacsbblogs.typepad.com/dataandresearch/ethics/

Drucker, P. (1946). Concept of the Corporation. The John Day Company.

Freedman, L. (2013). Strategy: A History. New York: Oxford University Press.

Hambrick, D. & Frederickson, J. (2001). Are you sure you have a strategy? Academy of Management Executive, 15: 48-59.

Henderson, B. (1989). The origin of strategy. Harvard Business Review, Nov-Dec: 139-143.

Ignatova, M. (2017). The Top 10 Buzzwords Recruiters Should Avoid. LinkIn Talent Blog. https://business.linkedin.com/talent-solutions/blog/linkedin-best-practices/2017/the-10-words-recruiters-should-not-put-on-their-linkedin-profiles-and-company-pages. Accessed 5/16/19.

Johnson, G. & Scholes, K. (1993). Exploring Corporate Strategy, 3rd ed. Hertfordshire, UK: Prentice-Hall International.

Katzenbach, J. & Smith, D. (1995). The discipline of teams. Harvard Business Review, March-April: 111-120.

Moffat, K & Zhang, A. (2014). The paths to social license to operate: An integrative model explaining community acceptance of mining. Resources Policy, 39: 61–70.

Mintzberg, H. (1987). Crafting strategy. Harvard Business Review, July. 2-11.

Mintzberg, H. (1992). Structure in fives: Designing Effective Organizations. Prentice-Hall.

Poundstone, W. (1992). Prisoner's Dilemma. New York: Doubleday.

Powell, T. (2017). Strategy as diligence: putting behavioral strategy into practice. California Management Review. Vol. 59(3) 162–190.

Selznick, P. (1957). Leadership in Administration: A Sociological Interpretation. Evanston, IL: Row & Peterson.

Starbucks website. http://www.starbucks.com/aboutus/pressdesc.asp?id=835. Accessed 8/20/08.

Wiersema, M. & Bantel, K. 1992. Top management team demography and corporate strategic change. Academy of Management Journal, 35: 91-121.

Chapter 2:
Industry & External Analysis

Chapter 1 addressed several definitions of strategy, the five elements that must be part of every strategy, and the characteristics of strategic decisions. It also covered how strategy differs from a company's mission and its vision. The importance of business ethics was also discussed. At the end of the chapter, the Strategy Process Cycle was presented. According to the model, the content of Chapter 1 should help leaders set and promote the company's strategic priorities. Hence, "priorities?" is the gate for passing from Setting Strategic Direction (Chpt. 1) to Analyze and Understand (Chpts 2 & 3).

Chapter 2 presents five powerful methods for understanding the industry and competitive environment that any organization is facing. We all know that today, industries are constantly changing, and they tend to be hyper-competitive. These two characteristics make it very difficult for a leader to create an effective strategy. By mastering the five methods presented in this chapter, a leader can be better equipped to understand the dynamism, competition, trends, and future of an industry. No single model or method can illuminate all the important aspects of an industry, but using the five presented below will illuminate key insights into any industry. By mastering them, a leader should be able to position a company to compete with its adversaries.

Learning Objectives for Chapter 2:

1. Learn which economic traits of an industry are important
2. Understand the Five Forces that influence the competitiveness of all industries
3. Recognize the Key Success Factors of an industry
4. Build a Strategic Group Map of an industry
5. Identify the Driving Forces that are changing the future of the industry

Opening Vignette for Chapter 2

For most leaders, the most difficult component of external analysis is *scenario planning,* which is imagining how the future will be different and how it will impact the company and the industry. The excerpt below is an example of using "industry foresight" to imagine how the customer of the future will be different than today. The last section of chapter 2 (Driving Forces Analysis) explains the concept in more detail.

2.2 Thought piece: an optimistic view of the customer of the future
Produced with the assistance of Ben Page, Ipsos MORI

2

2.2.1 The world in 2050

The global population has grown from 6.9 billion to 8.9 billion in the past 40 years. But birth rates in general, and particularly in the developed world, have continued to decline over the same period and radical new healthcare technologies have resulted in the average life expectancy in the developed world increasing to 99 years.

The global economy has also seen reasonably steady growth over the past 40 years, with the GDP of the G20 countries increasing from $38 trillion in 2009 to $170 trillion today. China became the world's largest economy just over 15 years ago and today China, India, Brazil, Russia and Mexico account for just over 50% of the GDP of the G20 countries. Indonesia, the Philippines, Vietnam, Iran, Turkey, Chile, and South Africa are not far behind.

New technology has revolutionized the way that people live their lives. Access to information in real time at any time of the day and anywhere on the planet is now a more widely held expectation. Virtually all people manage their lives using Lifestyle Integrated Management Pods (LIMPs), which are small portable devices containing all necessary personal data related to their owners. All LIMPs are allocated at birth and managed by parents until individuals reach 16 years of age.

LIMPs incorporate a real-time link to Internet 8, the global integrated communications and lifestyle management matrix. Through LIMPs, individuals can manage literally every part of their lives, including all communications, entertainment, business, commercial and information needs. They contain all bio-metric data and allow individuals to constantly monitor their own health and, to a certain extent, fix health problems that arise. They incorporate a means of contacting every other person on the planet that has their own LIMP. They facilitate the buying, selling and shipping of goods from any point to any destination and the ability to know precisely where those goods are every second of their journey. They provide a single portal for accessing all desired forms of electronic entertainment, including the ability to spend time in custom-designed or community-based virtual reality "lifestyles". They also provide access to information, including audio/video coverage, in real time of virtually every event that is taking place anywhere on the planet at any one time.

Both economic development and technological advances have changed the shape of global geopolitics for the better. After the turbulent period between 2010 and 2030, when tensions relating to ethnicity, religious beliefs and natural resources threatened to become unmanageable, global geopolitics have become generally more stable. Economic development in different parts of the world has generally resulted in greater economic parity amongst states, although the distinction between developed and developing still exists, and technology advances have facilitated real-time diplomacy. However, tensions between different states still exist over a number of issues. For example, concerns over fresh-water supplies are a cause of some tension even though 80% of the population now derives 80% of its drinking water from desalination plants. In addition, there are still disillusioned non-state-sponsored groups that are inclined to use violence to further their causes.

http://www.hbs.edu/faculty/Publication%20Files/IATA_Vision_2050_d4f5285f-63ed-4793-86e3-a3f6b0fd62cc.pdf

Introduction

Imagine that you are the coach of a basketball team. For your first game of the season, you want to prepare your team to play its best. As part of your preparation, your team practices shooting, passing, rebounding, defense, dribbling, and fitness. You have selected your five best players to start the game. Table 2.1 shows your roster and some characteristics of each player.

Table 2.1: Starting Team Basketball Roster

Position	Height	20 meter sprint
Point guard	5'5"	2.6 seconds
Shooting guard	5'8"	2.6 seconds
Forward / Post	5'10"	3.0 seconds
Forward / Post	5'10"	3.2 seconds
Center	6'1"	3.4 seconds

Given this information, would the coach be ready to prepare a strategy or game plan for his team? Take a few minutes and consider how you would approach the upcoming game. What game plan do you recommend?

When asked this question, many people make <u>assumptions</u> about the opponent, then design a strategy based on those assumptions. For example, did you assume that Table 2 described a professional team in the National Basketball Association? If so, your strategy would probably be irrelevant. Why? Because your team is probably too short and slow to be competitive against professionals. No matter what game plan you designed, this team would not be successful in a professional league. But if this were a high school girl's team, these players would be taller and faster than their average opponents. By now the point of this example is probably obvious. Specifically, the <u>context</u> of a strategy (or game plan) is critical. Until you know the details of your industry, it's impossible to create a meaningful strategy. A basketball coach would want to know the tendencies and abilities of an opponent, how it responds to different defenses, what strategies it prefers, etc.

The purpose of Chapter 2 is to introduce some techniques for managers to analyze their industry. By applying the techniques, managers will know the context of where they are competing and will be able to design an effective strategy with full knowledge of their opponents and other external forces that can impact profitability. For this book, the term "industry" refers to a collection of companies whose outputs are so similar that they compete for the same customers. Identifying the "boundaries" of an industry can be difficult, but there are clear pros and cons for defining an industry too broadly or too narrowly. As a starting point, you might consider the following questions. Is Coca-Cola a product in the "soft drink industry" or the "beverage industry?" After choosing one, describe the implications for that choice. For example, if you claim that the industry is "beverages," then who are the competitors in that industry with which Coca-Cola competes?

Chapter 2 is divided into five sections, with each section illustrating one method or technique for analyzing an industry. The five techniques are known as 1) Economic Conditions, 2) Five Forces Analysis, 3) Key Success Factors, 4) Strategic Group Analysis, and 5) Driving Forces Analysis. A manager who conducts all five of these techniques will have a comprehensive understanding of the competitive features of an industry. Chapter 2 explains step 2.a) of the Strategy Process Cycle (see Figure 1.3).

DOMINANT ECONOMIC CONDITIONS

The first step in industry analysis is to gather enough facts to create a thorough profile of the industry. Developing an economic profile is important because industries differ on many characteristics. Table 2.2 shows a list of characteristics in one column and the strategic implications in the other column.

Size of the Industry

Industry size is typically measured in dollars – the cumulative sales revenue of all the companies in the industry. Inflation can make it difficult to accurately compare years, so most industries also measure size in terms of unit volume of sales (the number of items sold in a year). For instance, the automobile industry reports sales in dollars and units sold for each quarter and each year. During 2014 about 16.4 million new cars and light trucks were sold (www.autoalliance.org) and the total revenue in the industry was around $550 billion. The implication of the size of the industry is that larger industries (> $1 billion) are typically dominated by large multinational companies. Furthermore, for any company to estimate is market share, it must know the size of the industry in which it competes.

Table 2.2: Economic Conditions of an Industry

Economic Condition	Strategic Implications
Size of the industry	▪ Largest industries attract large competitors but may contain unexploited niches. ▪ Largest industries tend to have more multinational competitors
Industry growth rate	▪ High growth makes competition less intense. ▪ But high growth can attract new entrants ▪ Can compare your company to industry avg. growth
Scope of rivalry	▪ Broad scope allows competitors from anywhere in the world.
Number of competitors	▪ Higher number indicates more competition.
Variability of customers	▪ More variability provides niche strategy options.
Degree of vertical integration	▪ Impacts rivals' operating cost structures. ▪ Impacts rivals' quality and volume control.
Types of distribution channels	▪ Impacts ability to sell to end users. ▪ Impacts cost structure of all competitors.
Economies of scale	▪ Allows some rivals to have lower unit costs. ▪ Discourages entrepreneurs from joining industry.
Speed of technological change	▪ Impacts R&D expenditures ▪ Can propel some companies to fast growth
Barriers to entry	▪ Determines the ease in which new companies can enter the industry.

Industry Growth Rate

The growth rate in an industry is usually measured as a *percentage change* in cumulative sale revenue from one period to another. See Figure 2.2 for a graph that compares the recent growth in the gaming industry to the film & music industry. The graph shows the gaming industry is bigger and growing faster. But how much faster? Look at the total revenue for the

Formula for % change: $\dfrac{value\ in\ period\ 2 - value\ in\ period\ 1}{value\ in\ period\ 1} \times 100$

Formula for CAGR: $\left(\dfrac{value\ at\ ending\ period}{value\ at\ beginning\ period}\right)^{\frac{1}{\#\ years}} - 1$

gaming industry: $122 billion in 2017 and then grew to $135 billion in 2018. According to the formula at the right, we calculate the growth rate as [(135-122) / 122] x 100 = 10.6%. For the film & musing industry, the one-year growth rate was [(60-58) / 58] x 100 = 3.4%. So we can conclude that in one year, the growth rate of gaming was about **triple the growth rate** of music & film. While it's important to know the one-year growth rate, a longer-term perspective is more important than a one-year view. The formula for the *compound annual growth rate* (CAGR) is a little more complicated. It shows the average growth rate over several periods of time. To use the formula, the results would be:

$$\left(\frac{135}{55}\right)^{\frac{1}{10}} - 1 \quad \rightarrow \quad (2.45)^{.1} - 1 \quad \rightarrow \quad 1.093 - 1 = \textbf{9.3\% compound annual growth rate}$$

Now we have good understanding of the gaming industry growth. It grew 10.6% during 2017 but over the last ten years, it has grown an average of about 9.3% every year. By looking at the bar graph, it appears the industry grew faster in the last five years. What was the growth rate from 2013 to 2018? To make a comparison, can you calculate the CAGR of the film & music industry for the last five and ten years?

Figure 2.2: Growth in Entertainment Industries

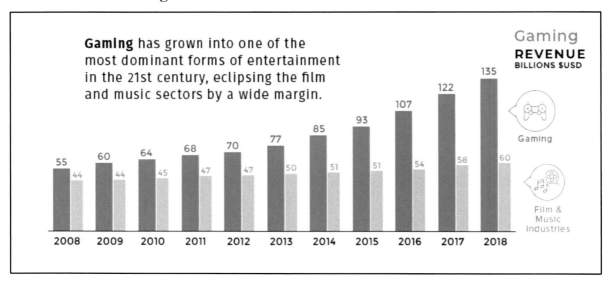

Source: https://www.visualcapitalist.com/esports-boom/

There are at least three implications of knowing the industry growth rate. First, we can compare it to the growth rate in the whole economy and to the inflation rate. Typically, the US economy grows between 2 and 4 percent per year and the annual inflation rate tends to be similar (see Figure 2.3). If an industry is growing slower than the economy and the inflation rate, it is considered to be less attractive to investors and potential new entrants. For managers of companies in slow growth industries, there must be conversations about the future of the industry. Is the slow growth expected to be a permanent feature of the industry, or is it only a temporary situation that can be turned around through investment and innovation? In the entertainment sector, growth in music and film has been lagging the economy for many years, and REALLY lagging the growth in the gaming industry. Will music and film ever return to their days of high growth, or has gaming become a more attractive and permanent replacement that many Americans have chosen? People are switching <u>away</u> from watching movies to playing PC games, cell phone games, and home platforms like Xbox and Wii. A second implication of the industry's growth rate is that it serves as a benchmark for managers of any company in the industry. For example, if you

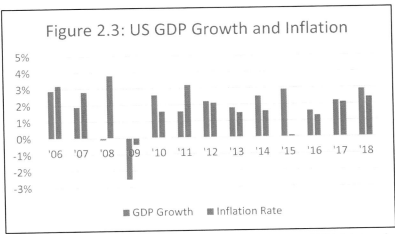

were the CEO of a company that makes video game software and your revenue was 10% higher in 2018 than in 2017, you might satisfied with that result. But when you realize that the industry grew a little faster during that time, you would know that your growth was only average, relative to your peers. If you are interested in more information about the gaming, film, and music industries, the end of the chapter shows another graph that compares the three.

Third, high growth industries usually attract the attention of companies that are looking for increased revenues. The high growth increases the odds that companies will enter the industry, hoping to grab a share of the revenue. Companies joining high growth industries is one reason we see "boom and bust" cycles occurring, such as the residential housing crisis beginning in 2007. When housing prices were rising, more and more builders joined the industry. At the same time, existing contractors built homes and condos to take advantage of high prices buyers were willing to pay. Soon there was a big oversupply of residential properties on the market so prices dropped. Many new homes remained empty for a long time, forcing some homebuilders into bankruptcy.

Scope of Rivalry and Number of Competitors

Industries vary on the extent to which competition is local, regional, national, or global. Most industries today are influenced by global trade, but some industries still are characterized by competition only at a local or regional level. E-commerce has encouraged the scope of competition to expand for many industries. For example, competition in many retail sectors was formerly local or regional. But e-commerce has encouraged retailers in many sectors to compete nationally or even globally (e.g. bookstores, clothing, and prescription medications). But other industries still see competition only at the local or regional level. Examples are service-based businesses like dry cleaning, restaurants, and any kind of home maintenance. Even some product-based businesses have managed to compete mostly with other regional competitors. Some examples are automobile dealerships, eyeglasses retailers, and grocery stores. The strategic implication of the scope of rivalry is probably obvious by now. Industries with global competition are more dynamic, less predictable, and usually more competitive than industries populated with only local competitors. For example, if you open a restaurant, you will be competing mostly against other restaurants in a small geographic area. If you open a bookstore, however, you will be competing with other bookstores in your area, but also against Amazon and other on-line retailers. The scope of competitive rivalry is much broader for some industries than others.

Variability of Customer

In some industries, the customers mostly buy and use the product in similar ways. In other industries, there is huge variability in how, why, and when customers buy and use the product. Specifically, in industries where the product is considered a staple or necessity item, customers tend to have a more uniform method of buying and using the product than in other industries. It's an obscure example for most people, but consider the wheat farming industry. Wheat is milled into flour, then sold to customers who fall into one (or more) groups: retailers (e.g. grocery stores) who buy in small packages for re-selling to consumers, restaurants who buy in commercial quantities for creating baked goods, and manufacturers who buy in massive quantities to make bread, pasta, pastries, etc. See Figure 2.4 for an overview of the distribution channels in the Australian wheat industry in 2006 (Spencer & Kneebone, 2007). Of all the wheat milled in Australia, 51% is distributed to the retail sector and then sold to consumers as bags of flour. Virtually all of those consumers will buy bags of flour in their local supermarket and use the flour in similar ways: baking at home. The second largest channel is industrial, which represents commercial bakeries that use flour to make bread, cookies, pastries, crackers, etc. Those customers buy in large quantities, require dependable delivery schedules, and usually request to be consulted about changes in how the wheat is grown and milled. The smallest channel is the restaurant industry, which buys flour for use in recipes such as bread, pasta, and desserts. These three customer groups have different demand volumes but only slightly different requirements for flour. Ultimately, the flour is used to make similar end products no matter which customer group is buying it. The demands of the customers within each group are likely to be similar. It's probably safe to assume that learning about customer demands, and meeting those demands, is mostly predictable.

Figure 2.4: Distribution in the Australian Wheat Industry, 2006

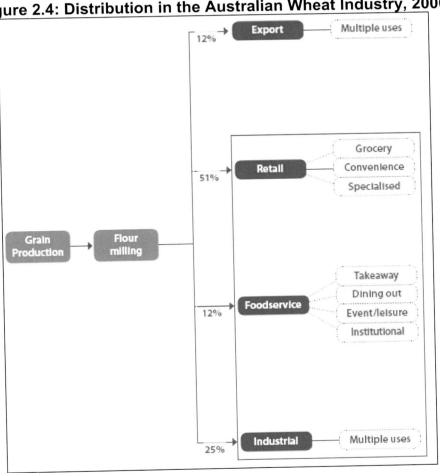

Now compare the wheat industry with the jetliner or the automobile industry. Companies like Boeing sell jets to governments, government agencies, air cargo companies (e.g FedEx) and airlines around the world. Each customer is likely to require customizations and features that are unique to each order.

Similarly, customers in the automobile industry often want to own distinctive cars. On most cars, there are hundreds of combinations of options available, and people like to further customize their vehicles after taking ownership. The point is that customers of the jetliner and automobile industries have much broader range of demands than customers of the wheat industry. In any industry, managers must be aware of the demand profile of customers, and the degree to which customer have different demands.

Degree of Vertical Integration

Vertical integration occurs when a company expands its operations to include activities that occur earlier or later in the chronological sequence of the industry activity chain. *Backward* vertical integration is when a company controls its suppliers or other inputs. *Forward* vertical integration is when a company owns or controls its distributors. A good example was provided by the Adolph Coors Company. In 1959 it became the first beverage company to use aluminum instead of steel cans. Soon after this aluminum can innovation, the company built the Coors Container Manufacturing plant. It was located on the same property as is brewery. The plant manufactured aluminum and glass containers that supplied the brewing company (and other companies) with beverage containers. This investment constitutes *backward* vertical integration because it was an investment in an activity farther removed from the end user. Another instance of backward vertical integration at Coors was the company's investment in its barley procurement and breeding program. Like other brewers, Coors bought barley from farmers, but the company also had its own staff of agricultural scientists who researched the development of new strains of barley that might enable the company to gain an advantage in taste, cost, etc. The company also created the Coors Transportation Company, which designed and owned a fleet of refrigerated trucks that could deliver Coors beer from the brewery directly to retailers. Coors was the first company to claim that its beer was maintained in a temperature-controlled environment from the moment it was brewed until the time it was delivered to a refrigerator at a retailer's store or warehouse. This investment was an example of *forward* vertical integration because it was an activity that occurred nearer in time to the end user's purchase of the product.

Figure 2.5 provides an illustration of the Coors business model before and after the vertical integration was completed. In each panel of the figure, the shaded boxes indicate the activities in the brewing industry that Coors controlled. In the left panel (before vertical integration) only one box is shaded. At that time in its history, Coors was involved in only brewing beer. In the right hand side of the figure, three boxes are shaded. By this time in its history Coors had completed its backward and forward vertical integration. Instead of buying cans and bottles from suppliers, Coors made its own beverage containers. In fact, by 1990, Coors had become so good at manufacturing aluminum cans that it was the largest producer in the world – about 4 billion cans annually! And instead of contracting with a trucking company to deliver its beer to retailers, Coors developed its own fleet of refrigerated tractor trailers. As with the other "economic conditions" described in this section, we now turn to explaining the strategic implications of vertical integration. A good starting point would be to examine the strengths and weaknesses for pursuing vertical integration. Later in the book – in the section on Corporate Level Strategy in chapter 4 – we will discuss how vertical integration fits with the whole of a company's enterprise strategy.

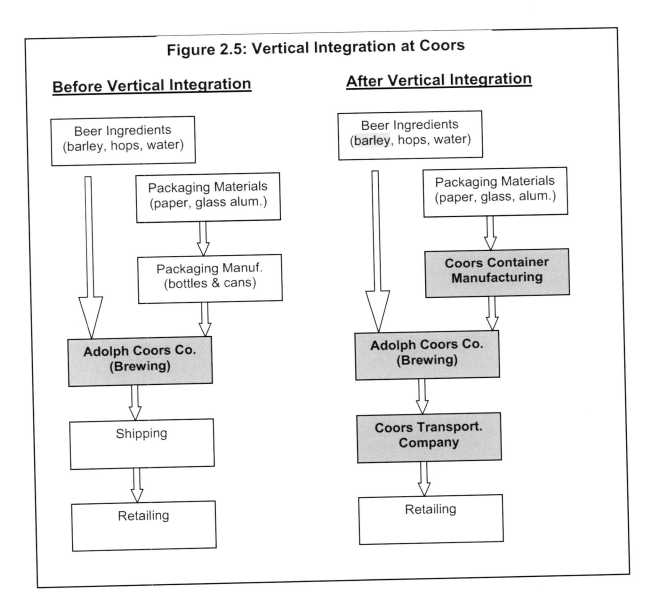

Figure 2.5: Vertical Integration at Coors

Strengths of Vertical Integration

- Reduced operating costs – If a company buys its supplies and inputs on the open market, it will pay a price that includes a profit margin to the supplier. If the company pursues backward vertical integration, it can usually make the item for a lower unit cost than it pays the supplier.

- Better control of quantity and quality – If a company buys its supplies and inputs on the open market, it can be susceptible to shortages in the market and quality control problems from its vendors. Backward vertical integration can give a company better control of its supply chain because it becomes less dependent on companies that supply key inputs.
- Potential new source of revenue – The Adolph Coors Company built a can manufacturing plant with a capacity larger than it needed to supply its own demand for cans. With the excess capacity, Coors sold aluminum cans to other beverage manufacturers. Coors could operate the factory at full capacity (to keep per unit costs as low as possible), use the cans it needed for its own beer brands, and sell the leftover cans as a source of additional revenue.

<u>Weaknesses of Vertical Integration</u>

- High capital costs - Certainly in the example of Coors, vertical integration was a capital intensive strategy. Designing and building a new manufacturing facility can cost over $100 million. To approve a project of that size, managers must be willing to take a long-term view that allows the project to earn at least the company's cost of capital.
- Development of new competencies – Beverage containers (bottles & cans) are necessary for the beer industry. However, the manufacturing of beverage containers requires wholly different resources and competencies than brewing beer. For many companies, the addition of a new business creates complexities that are too big to manage easily.

Types of Distribution Channels

Many industries have unique systems for how products are moved from manufacturers to shippers to wholesalers to retailers. To be competitive in an industry, managers must understand the "rules" and nuances of the distribution system that dictate how products move. A few industries have competitors that are fully vertically integrated, like ExxonMobil. In those cases, the company has fewer relationships to manage (with suppliers or distribution partners) than a company that must negotiate with vendors, customers, product brokers, and distribution partners. Even gaining access to distribution channels can be difficult task in many industries. Powerful companies intentionally restrict access to the distribution system (usually via exclusive contracts) so that 1) competitors will struggle to make products available to customers or 2) vendors will be required to pay fees to gain access to the distribution system. A good example is how supermarkets have developed the practice of charging "slotting fees" to food manufacturing companies. The Federal Trade Commission has studied the practice since it began in the 1970s. Slotting fees

> "are one-time payments a supplier makes to a retailer as a condition for the initial placement of the supplier's product on the retailer's store shelves or for initial access to the retailer's warehouse space. Every year, suppliers propose thousands of new grocery products, each competing for retail grocery store shelf space. To decide whether to stock a new product, retailers engage in complex and multi-faceted discussions and negotiations with suppliers" (Federal Trade Commission, 2003:5).

When a food manufacturer wants to introduce a new product, it must plan for distributing the new product via supermarkets. Because shelf space is a scarce and crucial resource in the food distribution system, supermarkets can demand these slotting fees from manufacturers who want some shelf space. According to the FTC report, a food manufacturer should expect to spend between $1 million and $2 million in slotting fees to introduce a new product nationally. In a study published in Forbes, Copple found "for a new product the standard price of admission to the shelves is a slotting fee—up to $25,000 per item for a regional cluster of stores. (A California food producer says he met with a buyer at a chain grocer who demanded $250,000 for ten stores and wouldn't even take a meeting until he received a $100,000 check.) Small manufacturers hate paying upfront money; it can put them out of business before they've even started" (Copple, 2002).

While slotting fees are unique to the supermarket industry, other industries have unique distribution channel characteristics that must be mastered by successful companies. Consider the restaurant industry. In 2012, the distribution system for restaurants was complicated, but well-known: customer arrives at the restaurant, orders food, waits for the food, and then consumes it. Adding a drive-thru window or a delivery service was an added complexity, but was already integrated into the demand and production system. Then, in 2014, UberEats arrived on the scene. People began using UberEats (and Grub Hub, etc) instead of going to a restaurant and instead of going to the grocery store. For restaurants, this innovation in the distribution of food helped restaurants boots their sales *quantity*, but it reduced their profit margins. Is this a good trade-off? Keng (2018) is not sure. His article is titled "Why Uber Eats Will Eat You Into Bankruptcy" and describes the economics for restaurants that participate in the newest method of distribution in the industry.

Economies of Scale

In some industries, economies of scale explain big differences between companies. For managers in any company, it is important to be aware whether these differences exist. Economies of scale exist when a company is able to lower its total unit costs in the long run by engaging in bulk production of its goods or services. Over time, a company that captures economies of scale will develop a cost advantage over competitors in its industry. Figure 2.6 is a graph that should look familiar from an economics course. It compares Average Total Cost (AC), Average Fixed Cost (AFC), and Average Variable Cost (AVC). As shown in the graph, the company's cost per unit (AC) decreases as the quantity of production increases (x-axis). This inverse relationship continues until about the point when production hits about 13,000 units.

Figure 2.6: Illustration of Economies of Scale

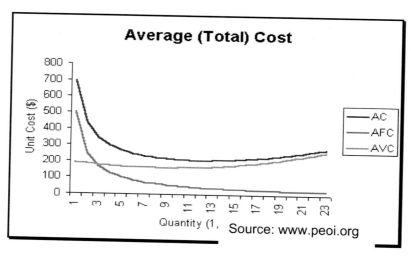

Source: www.peoi.org

Each company in an industry has a total cost curve unique to its cost structure. The company that keeps the lowest cost structure in the industry has an advantage over its competitors. Of course there may be other advantages that other firms develop, and other methods for cutting costs, but economies of scale is a good explanation for why some companies develop a cost leadership position. The reason economies of scale occurs is that a portion of total costs are fixed, as shown by the green line (AFC) in Figure 2.5. Examples of fixed costs are rent and insurance premiums. Those costs do not vary as production increases. So as production volume increases, the fixed cost per unit decreases. This pattern continues indefinitely, as shown by the AFC line moving closer to zero as production increases.

As mentioned earlier, the lowest point on the AC curve occurs at about 12,000 units of production. After that point, AC begins to rise due to *diseconomies* of scale. Diseconomies can occur because of difficulty in efficiently managing an increasingly large operation. Up to a point, "bigger is better" but past that point the large size of an operation becomes unwieldy and causes breakdown in administration and communication.

Sources of Information about Industries

Understanding all the economic conditions and facts of an industry is only the first step. The second step is knowing where to find the relevant information that will help create a full profile of the industry. If a person wants to know the economic traits of the restaurant industry, where should he look? The most obvious source would be the popular search engines on the internet, like Google, Bing, and Yahoo. Most search engines obtain information from original sources, so another method would be to find those sources. Most industries have created a non-profit organization called a "trade association" to help support and promote the industry. Depending on its size and complexity, most trade associations have full-time paid employees whose role is to do public relations for the industry, promote its members, collect information about the industry and monitor its health, and maybe encourage legislative action that benefits the industry (e.g. lobby Congress to pass laws that the industry supports). Most trade associations have a website that provides some free information about the status of the industry. Returning to our question about the restaurant industry, we can discover that there are several trade associations that support and provide information about restaurants: National Restaurant Association, American Institute of Wine and Food, International Hotel & Restaurant Association.

Another category of sources of industry information is market research companies. IBIS World and Datamonitor are companies that conduct research on industries, then make the reports available via subscription or pay-per-report fees. Many university libraries subscribe to one of these systems so the reports can be accessed by students and faculty.

Third, many financial analysts and brokerage companies produce reports on publicly traded companies. The reports are focused on evaluating the stock price and the equity value of a company, but they usually also contain commentary, insights, and facts about the industry. Similarly, the rating agencies produce reports on companies that can contain useful information about industries and their competitive outlook. Examples are Moody's and Standard & Poor's.

Summary

Table 2.2 contains a representative list of economic conditions that might be useful for understanding any industry. Certainly there are other facts that might be important for a specific industry. For instance, competitors in the airline industry monitor Available Seat Miles (ASM), which is a measure of supply in the industry. Specifically, it is the number of available passenger seats in the industry multiplied by the number of miles flown over a given time (month or year). Other industries have their own specific metrics or economic conditions that have been designed to present key data. Most industries have at least one trade association that is responsible for collecting industry data and making it available to members of the association, the press, and government agencies that request it. Trade associations are a good place to start for people who are searching for information about a specific industry.

FIVE FORCES ANALYSIS

In section one of this chapter, we examined the *economic* conditions that must be understood as a precursor to developing strategy. Similarly, every industry has unique *competitive* conditions also. For many years, the most prevalent method for studying the competitive conditions in an industry has been the "Five Forces Model." Originally developed by Porter (1980), the model is based on the recognition that competitors in any industry are subject to the same five forces. The forces might be more or less powerful in different industries and might have different impact on specific companies, but they are germane and influential in every industry. Figure 2.7 illustrates the Five Forces Model.

The goal of conducting a Five Forces analysis is to draw a conclusion about the competitive rigor in an industry. The centerpiece in the model mentions "rivalry among existing firms." Some industries are characterized by intense rivalry while others industries have a degree of competitive insulation, which makes competition less intense. The implication of each of the five forces is that when the forces are strong, they tend to suppress profits in the industry. In the following section, each of the five forces is discussed.

Figure 2.7: The Five Force Model

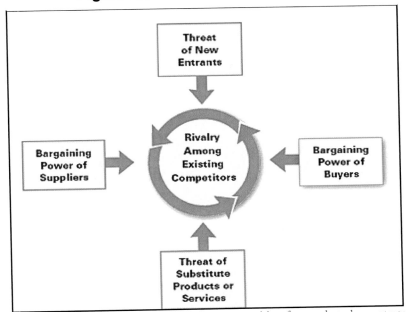

Source: https://hbr.org/2008/01/the-five-competitive-forces-that-shape-strategy

Threat of New Entrants

Estimating the threat of new entrants is important because new entrants represent potential lost market share for companies already competing in the industry. If new entrants can join the industry and manage to establish a foothold in the market, then they will attract some customers that probably could have been acquired by the incumbent companies. Whether new entrants represent a serious threat depends primarily on the industry's barriers to entry, which are any strategic or economic "hurdles" that a company must overcome if it wants to join the industry. According to Porter (1980) there are several types of barriers to entry.

- **Economies of scale** can be a barrier to entry because strong scale economies often give incumbent companies a cost advantage over new entrants. See Figure 2.6 for a review of economies of scale. If existing companies have established an advantage based on economies of scale, a new entrant has a choice among two difficult options. First, the new entrant can enter the industry on a large scale (comparable to the competitors) in hopes of achieving a low cost operation. This option is difficult because it usually requires a large capital investment and can create over-capacity problems. Trying this approach means a new entrant must start its existence while pretending to be a large company Second, the new entrant might prefer to start on a small scale but then faces a cost disadvantage compared to the existing companies that have already achieved economies of scale. Either way, a new entrant has a barrier that it must overcome if scale economies are powerful in an industry.

- **Strong customer loyalty** creates a barrier to entry because it means that customers in an industry are rarely willing to switch providers of the good or service that they are consuming. When potential new entrants realize that customers tend to be brand loyal, they may be discouraged from trying to enter the industry only to struggle to gain market share.

- **Cost disadvantages independent of size** can occur because incumbent companies have lower costs that are not based on their size. For example, a new entrant may not be able to acquire raw materials at favorable prices because long term contracts exist that favor older, more established companies. Or, there may be a shortage of labor in the industry so that a new entrant must pay above-market wages to hire new employees. These are just two examples of situations that can cause new entrants to incur higher costs than incumbent companies.

- **Limited access to distribution channels** restrict the number of customers that a new entrant can serve. Earlier in this chapter, the supermarket industry practice of charging "slotting fees" was described as an example of an economic condition. This practice is clearly an example of an entry barrier that reduces the likelihood that a company can successfully join this industry. If a start-up company has a great new food product but can't manage to get it onto the supermarket shelves, consumers may never be able to easily buy it. Distribution channels can also be restricted by exclusive contracts. For example many universities are either a "Pepsi campus" or a "Coke campus." All vending machines and food service shops are contracted to one exclusive provider. Such contracts might span several years, during which time no other beverage manufacturers are allowed to compete on the campus.

- **Government regulation** can create a barrier to entry in many ways. Probably the most common example is when a government requires an organization (or a sole practitioner) to have a license or permit before commencing operations. For example, a lawyer must pass the bar exam in the state where he practices, and have a license to practice law there. Consumers usually believe the government is wise to require such permission so that they have some protection against unscrupulous business owners or practitioners. Another common way that a government can create an entry barrier is through import tariffs or taxes. The US Government has enacted a tariff on ethanol imported from Brazil. Each gallon of ethanol is subjected to a tariff of $.54 (De Gorter & Just, 2008). The tariff creates an incentive for American producers of ethanol and a barrier to entry for Brazilian manufacturers who are considering exporting their product to US. Brazilian producers must add the cost of the tariff to their total costs. Some might conclude that the tariff makes their product too costly to export to the US. Third, governments sometimes create territorial restrictions that grant a local monopoly to one company, or severely restrict the amount of competition in a region. Most local utilities (e.g. electricity) are companies that are regulated by a division of the state government. The utility company agrees to have its prices regulated by the government, and the government prevents any other company from competing with the utility company.

This list of entry barriers is not exhaustive. Many other barriers can exist. After the barriers to entry have been identified, managers can assess the threat of new entrants. When entry barriers are numerous and high, the threat of new entrants is decreased. On the other hand, low entry barriers tend to make an industry more susceptible to entrance by new companies. As an example, most cities have hundreds of companies listed in the business directory for the "management consulting" industry. Virtually anyone can claim to be a management consultant because no industry certifications are required to prove a person has expertise.

Threat of Substitute Products

Substitute products (or services) meet the same need as the solutions from the target industry, but they *originate from another industry*. Coca-Cola and Dr. Pepper <u>are not</u> substitute products but are competing products – they are competing against each other in the soft drink industry. Instead, orange juice is one of many substitutes for Coca-Cola. The second step in the 5 Forces Analysis is to evaluate the relative threat of substitute products. After identifying the names of the substitutes, a manager should then determine how threatening they are. The threat is determined by two features: the quality of the substitution and the switching costs that the buyer incurs when he switches to the substitute. The quality of the substitution is a subjective comparison of the products in the two industries. As an example, consider the automobile industry. When a person buys an automobile, what need is being met? That is the first question that must be answered to determine the threat of a substitute product. For most customers, a car meets the need for transportation, so a potential substitute product is a bicycle. But the quality of substitution that a bicycle provides is not very high for most people who need transportation. Compared to a car, a bicycle is slower, more dangerous, provides no protection from bad weather, and has low storage capacity. The main benefit is that a bicycle is much cheaper to operate and doesn't cause pollution. Of course, this is is a simplistic analysis meant only to illustrate that the quality of the substitute must be assessed. A more thorough analysis of the car vs. bike switching cost would consider many other details. For example, this analysis began with the assumption that the purpose of a car is to provide transportation. For some people, a car also provides *prestige* in addition to transportation. In that case, riding a bicycle could never be a good substitute product.

Second, to assess switching costs, we must consider the <u>costs</u> a buyer incurs when switching from one provider to another. To switch from a car to a bicycle requires low financial costs (cost of acquisition and cost of operating are both higher for a car), but there are non-financial costs to consider also. There is a cost of training to ride a bicycle for distances that can replace a commute to work or school and the cost of taking longer to commute to work. These are low switching costs but are not usually low enough to make bicycles a threatening substitute to the automobile. Taken together, the quality of the substitute and the switching costs are not compelling to make most people ride a bike for transportation.

One last point should be made about the threat of substitutes: they create a <u>price ceiling</u> for the target industry. Imagine a person who prefers sugar instead of artificial sweeteners in his coffee. These are substitute products because they originate from different industries, but they meet the same purpose. If for some reason the price of sugar increases substantially, then the substitute becomes a bit more attractive. At some point, the consumer might decide that the price of sugar has risen too high, and he would switch to an artificial sweetener. This point is known as the price ceiling because it represents the maximum the consumer is willing to pay before he switches to an alternative solution. Normally, price ceilings are defined as a price which is set artificially low by a government restriction. Most power utility companies have a local monopoly, and they are restricted from raising prices without local government approval.

Bargaining Power of Suppliers / Vendors

Suppliers (or vendors) to an industry are companies that provide the inputs or raw materials to companies in the industry. For example in the grocery store industry, suppliers are food manufacturing companies such as Kraft Foods, General Mills, and The Coca-Cola Company. To evaluate the bargaining power of suppliers to an industry, several situations must be considered. These situations all play a role in influencing the power that suppliers can have. To conclude that a supplier is powerful indicates that it is able to dictate terms of transactions with its customers. More powerful companies are able to negotiate more favorable terms than less powerful ones.

- Size of supplier – As a general rule, the larger the supplier (in terms of gross annual revenue) the more powerful the supplier will be.

- Number of suppliers – In cases where the number of suppliers to an industry shrinks, the remaining suppliers are usually more powerful than they were before the contraction. For example, consider a situation where there are five suppliers to an industry. If companies 1 and 2 merge, then there will be three companies remaining. On average, those three companies will be more powerful than the five that existed before the mergers. In 1996 Union Pacific and Southern Pacific railroads announced plans to merge. The merger eventually created the largest railroad in the US but at the time of the announcement, the merger was opposed by the US Justice Department. "Denying the merger was 'the most certain, effective and expeditious way to preserve competition'. It said, for example, that reduced competition could cost shippers as much as $800 million a year in higher prices" (Bryant, 1996). The Justice Department was concerned that the merged railroad would be so powerful that it would be able to unfairly raise prices for its customers. A more recent example occurred when the FCC opposed the merger between the cell phone carriers T-Mobile and AT&T in 2011. "Had AT&T acquired T-Mobile, consumers in the wireless marketplace would have faced higher prices and reduced innovation" (De la Merced, 2011). The FCC believed that if it allowed the number of suppliers to shrink, the remaining suppliers would be too powerful to provide fair competition in the market.

- Importance of supplied inputs – Independent of the size of the suppliers, some inputs that are purchased are more important than others. The more important the inputs, the more powerful are the vendors who provide the input. To the automobile industry, steel is much more important than copper. Most of the body, frame, transmission, and engine are made of steel. While fiberglass and aluminum can be used to make the body and engine respectively, steel continues to be the predominant raw material. Usually the electrical wiring in a car is made from copper, but the volume of copper will always be much lower than steel. Furthermore, aluminum can be used as an excellent substitute for copper wiring. So when we analyze the automobile industry, the suppliers of steel are much more powerful than the suppliers of copper, all other factors being equal. Steel represents a significant proportion of a car's total cost of materials, so steel suppliers are in a powerful negotiating position relative to the car makers.

Another reason the supplied inputs can be important is due to their uniqueness, independent of their proportion of total costs. Returning to the example from the automobile industry, tires illustrate this point. To the car makers, tires represent a small part of the total cost of the car, but there are no feasible substitutes for the modern rubber-based tire. Of course there several companies that manufacture tires and compete for the car makers' business. But they all have some bargaining leverage because they provide an essential part of the car's design.

A more recent example of powerful vendors is illustrated in the escalating trade friction between the US and China. Rare earth minerals are critical components to many modern technology products, ranging from cell phones to electric car batteries. The US imports about 80% of its rare earth minerals from China (Figure 2.8). In response to tariffs imposed by the Trump administration, China has threatened to restrict its export of rare earth minerals. With few alternative suppliers, some American companies could feel the impact of this threat of suppliers (Bloomberg, 2019). If China decides to reduce or stop the supply, American companies don't have many alternative sources that can provide the same quantity of rare earth minerals without a long advance warning. Suppliers can be a powerful force for service-based industries too, especially in the case of the supply of labor. Labor intensive businesses are sensitive to increases in wage rates. When labor shortages occur, existing employees are able negotiate better deals because they have a scare resource (their own job skills) employees must obtain.

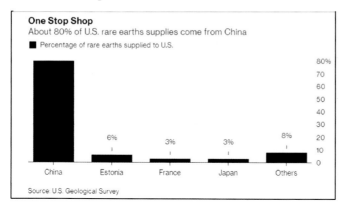

Figure 2.8:
US Dependence on Rare Earth Minerals

Bargaining Power of Customers / Buyers

Customers (or buyers) are consumers and companies that buy the outputs of the industry being analyzed. Customers must perceive that a product or service creates good value for them or they would probably discontinue buying it. So if customers become unhappy (they perceive that are receiving less value than before) and if they are powerful, they may be able to demand price concessions or changes in future transactions. The question in view is: are individual customers powerful enough to change the terms of the deal? There are several conditions that influence the relative power of customers to an industry. More powerful customers make an industry more competitive, and hence, less attractive to the industry incumbents.

- Proportion of output that customers buy – The larger portion of total output that a customer buys, the more powerful that customer becomes. For example, if a customer buys 80% of a company's output it will be in a more powerful position than a customer that buys only 5% of the output.

- Size of the customer – Considering the size of the customer (in total revenue) independent of other factors, a larger customer is usually more powerful than a smaller customer. Larger customers tend to have more demanding requirements for exact specifications on procurement details, delivery schedule, product/service features, and price breaks for volume. If the customer buys a large portion of output, these demands are difficult to ignore. In the late 1990s Dell Computer Corporation was streamlining its supply chain. It demanded that its suppliers of computer components open a facility nearby its three assembly plants in Austin, TX, Limerick, Ireland, and Penang, Malaysia. As the customer, Dell clearly had strong bargaining power in these relationships. In order to keep Dell as a customer, the components suppliers agreed to open facilities to meet Dell's demand for speedy delivery (McWilliams, 1997).

- Ability to backward vertically integrate – Customers that have the financial, technical, and strategic resources to backward vertically integrate will have more bargaining power than those that cannot backward vertically integrate.

Competitive Rivalry in the Industry

The last of the five forces to assess is the one shown in the middle of Figure 2.7. How do we determine the amount of rivalry in an industry? It is influenced by all four of the forces described above. The stronger each of those forces, the more intense the rivalry in the industry. Furthermore, the intensity of the rivalry is also influenced by other factors independent of those four forces.

Specifically, 1) the industry growth rate, 2) the industry structure, and 3) the height of the exit barriers in the industry all influence the strength of rivalry in an industry.

The industry growth rate is important because it influences how companies seek to earn revenue growth. When an industry is declining (or showing nominal growth) companies often resort to "stealing" customers and market share from competitors. They engage in price wars, head-to-head comparisons, and benchmarking in an effort to gain any small and/or temporary advantage in the market. As a group, these tactics have been called "strategic herding" (Nattermann, 2000). They tend to help a company's performance in the short run because they position the company in the largest part of the market. But according to Natterman's data, the longer term effect is to reduce profit margins throughout the industry. As firms in an industry become more similar over time, they crowd into a similar space and find success to be more elusive. Conversely, when the industry is growing, companies tend to be more focused on meeting capacity demands, gaining new loyal customers, and building a resource base to meet growth forecasts. They are less intent on fighting each other for small market share gains. So a growing industry tends to create less intense competition than a declining one.

Industry structure refers to the number of firms in an industry. At one end of the continuum is a monopoly –there is only on firm so there is no competition. For that one competition is not an issue at all. The other end of the continuum is known as perfect competition: there are many firms of equal size, capabilities, and information. We would not expect any firm to be able to create a permanent competitive advantage, so competition is the most intense it can be.

Exit barriers are the inverse of entry barriers. They make it difficult for firms to leave an industry. A common exit barrier is the cost associated with dissolution of assets. If a firm has invested in assets that are specialized or have a single use, there might not be a market in which the firm can liquidate them. For instance, consider a firm that has spent millions of dollars to develop a specialized assembly line. If the firm is losing money, managers may consider closing the company and exiting the industry. But if they discover that it is nearly impossible to sell the company's assets, they might elect to keep the business open instead of incurring the sure loss of abandoning the assets. Another common exit barrier is a contract or a lease agreement. In early 2019, Tesla announced that it would close almost all of its 106 retail stores and galleries in 26 states. The decision was motivated by the need to save money on real estate costs and focus instead on selling cars on-line only. However, "landlords could seek a court injunction to prevent Tesla from closing stores before the lease expiration" (Fung, 2019:B1). Other famous retailers like Starbuck's and Kenneth Cole have not been allowed to close stores in malls, even when the stores were performing poorly. When exit barriers are high in an industry, there tends to be over-capacity because firms rarely leave. Instead, they stay in the industry and continue to retain some market share. This situation creates higher competition.

After examining the forces that influence the level of competition, the next step in external analysis is to consider commonalities among competitors in the industry.

KEY SUCCESS FACTORS

In every industry, there are standards that emerge as the industry becomes more mature. Some standards occur because of laws (e.g. physicians must be licensed before they practice medicine) and others occur because one dominant design or industry standard becomes common and expected. The early cell phones had only a basic camera. Nobody expected for their cell phones to replace a "real" camera, so it was common for people to carry both a camera and a cell phone while traveling. As cell phones became more advanced, having an excellent camera became expected. Today, it is safe to say that an excellent camera is a KSF for the cell phone industry. A handset can't really be competitive unless it contains an excellent camera. Other standards describe strategic decisions and actions that firms must take. Altogether these standards are known as key success factors (KSFs) – they are the behaviors, competencies, or characteristics that are required of companies to stay competitive in an industry. Mastery of KSFs do not guarantee success, but the absence of KSFs do indicate that a company will not stay competitive for long. The definition of KSFs is typically outside the control of any company. Instead, they are dictated by customers, competitors, and governments – they are norms established by the industry constituents. As an example, consider the supermarket industry. An obvious KSF is cleanliness because customers want to buy their food from a place they believe to be safe for food handling and storage. If they find that a grocery store is unclean they will not be likely to return to that store. If a grocery store is clean (i.e. it has mastered this KSF) it could still go out of business. But without cleanliness, failure is certain. Now consider gasoline retailing. Cleanliness is not too important for most customers, but convenience is probably a KSF. Most people recognize that there are not big differences in the quality of gasoline between the brand name gas stations. And there is not much difference on prices in a local market, so convenience has become a KSF for this industry. People prefer to pay at the pump, have easy access to the pumps, and have good parking, and speedy checkout service if they want to make purchases.

For any industry, there are only a handful of KSFs. The trick is to identify the standards for the industry, rather than strategy features of individual companies. The temptation is to think "The KSF for ACB Company is _____." Instead, KSFs should be identified by understanding what all customers in an industry demand from providers. KSFs could be attributes of the product or service, or delivery methods, or other competencies that are "non-negotiable". Once the KSFs have been identified, they can be used as benchmarks for comparing to the strategy of companies in the industry.

As an example of identifying KSFs and then comparing companies to them, consider the retail consumer electronics industry. For most retail industries, <u>location</u> is a KSF. In November 2008 Circuit City (the large electronics retailer) filed for bankruptcy protection. Some reports blamed Circuit City's failure on the recession. But according to Hamilton (2008), Circuit City filed for bankruptcy because "The problems began a decade ago, when Circuit City failed to secure prime real estate — its out-of-the-way locations were often just inconvenient enough to tempt customers to head to other retailers, like Wal-Mart." If his conclusions are correct, Hamilton illustrated that Circuit City ignored a KSF in its industry, and eventually failed because of it. Circuit City and Best Buy were both founded in the early 1980s. While Best Buy was opening its stores in the best locations, Circuit City was stuck with older sites with less convenient access. As the industry matured, Best Buy grew faster and avoided the financial problems that began to plague Circuit City beginning in 2006. According to Hamilton's analysis (2008), Best Buy's management team adhered more closely to the KSFs for the consumer electronics retailing industry.

STRATEGIC GROUP ANALYSIS

In every industry, some competitors are more similar than others. Companies that have similar strategies and approaches are said to be in the same "strategic group". For example, if a woman wants to buy a new dress she can shop at Wal-Mart, which is the market share leader in the apparel industry. Wal-Mart sells more clothing than any retailer in the US. Instead, the woman could shop at Nordstrom for her new dress. As most people realize, those two retailers do not compete very closely with each other. The products, the image, the suppliers, the locations, and the target markets are all different. Although Wal-Mart and Nordstrom are both competing in the retail apparel industry, they are not in the same strategic group. They both sell clothing, but they do not compete for the same customers too often. Knowing the members of the strategic groups in an industry helps manages develop strategy for competing with rivals in the industry.

Most industries contain several strategic groups. Part of analyzing any industry is to realize the nature and composition of those groups. To that end, we can create a "strategic group map" to illustrate the relative position of companies in an industry. Figure 2.9 is a strategic group map of the local pizza industry for Tampa, FL. The steps for creating a strategic group map are below.

Creating a Strategic Group Map

1. Identify the most important competitive characteristics of companies in the industry. This list of characteristics should include some Key Success Factors (see previous section) but should also identify some characteristics that distinguish some companies from others. The characteristics should describe differences in how companies have developed their strategies. After the list has been made, choose two characteristics and use one as the x-axis label and the other as the y-axis label on the map. The two characteristics chosen in Figure 2.9 were *convenience* and *variety of toppings / flavors*. There are certainly other reasons why customers choose one pizza brand over another. Drawing a map with these two axes will be useful, and then another map can be drawn using different labels. Also, the two characteristics should have a low correlation. In other words, they should not vary together. When the labels on each axis do have a high correlation, all the companies on the map will appear along a diagonal line from the lower left corner to the upper right corner. Imagine if we chose *price* and *quality* as our two axes. In most situations, companies that have the highest quality products also have the highest price while companies with the lowest prices usually have lower quality.

Figure 2.9: Strategic Group Map – Tampa Pizza Industry

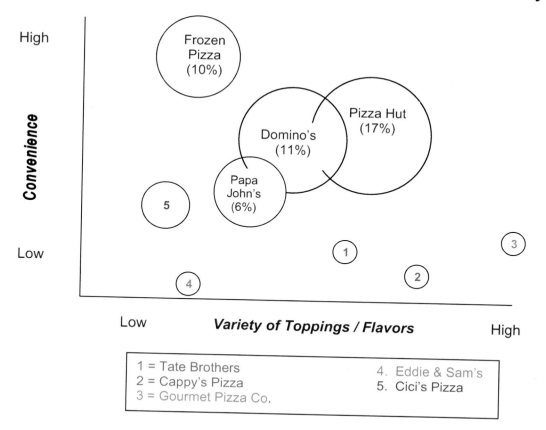

2. Make a list of the companies in the industry that should be included on the strategic group map. For each company also estimate the market share that it controls. In section 2 of this chapter (5 Forces Analysis) the concept of substitute products was introduced. Notice that in Figure 2.9, one of the circles is "frozen pizza". This entry might be a substitute instead of a competitor, but the strict definitions of substitutes vs. competitors is less important in this analysis.

3. Evaluate each company on the list according to it how well it performs on the two criteria that were identified in step #1.

4. Draw a circle on the map to represent the placement of each company in the industry. The size of the circle should estimate the company's market share.

Once the map has been drawn, it should be interpreted. One way to understand the implications of a strategic group map is to answer questions about its characteristics. The following questions apply to Figure 2.9.

- How many strategic groups exist?

The big three national chains are an obvious strategic group. They are positioned (literally) in the middle of the markey and appeal to the most number of consumers. Cici's Pizza is a smaller franchise chain that has fewer locations (so less convenient) and is typically a low cost alternative. According to this map, Cici's looks to be alone in its own strategic group. Third, the frozen pizzas available in grocery and convenience stores represent a unique strategic group. They are usually of lower quality taste than a restaurant-made pizza, but they offer the best convenience (assuming that they are purchased in advance and are available in your freezer at home). The fourth strategic group contains the locally owned pizza restaurants. Most of these providers have only one location and offer limited delivery, so they are rated as having lower convenience than the national chains. However, they are known for having the most creative recipes, specialty toppings, and regional influences. They are spread across the x-axis, but they are probably all in the same strategic group.

- Which strategic group is likely to be the most competitive?

As in most industries, the strategic group that is most popular with customers is the one that is the most crowded with competitors. Consequently, the largest strategic group (Pizza Hut, Domino's, Papa Johns) is probably the most competitive.

- Where are the "white spaces" in the industry?

One of the main benefits of creating an accurate strategic group map is that it illustrates "white spaces" in an industry. These spaces indicate opportunities that might be pursued by one or more companies that identify them. However, in some maps, some regions are strategically unattractive. In Figure 2.6 the lower left region is probably not an attractive region for any consumers because it would describe a pizza provider that had very low convenience and very few toppings or flavors. In contrast, most of the right side of the map is vacant. This vacancy suggests that there might be an opportunity for a company to provide convenience similar to (or better than) Pizza Hut but offer more flavor varieties.

- What strategic changes could we expect in the industry?

We could forecast plausible strategic changes for several companies in the industry. First, Papa John's is the smallest of the large companies, probably because it trails its strategic group in both convenience and perceived pizza quality. We might expect to see Papa John's try to shift to the right on the x-axis: offer a broader menu with more varieties of toppings and flavors. Second, companies in the frozen segment might attempt a similar re-positioning. Freezer space in the supermarkets is a precious resource, so companies might go "upmarket" to higher quality, higher priced pizzas that earn higher profit margins. This might be accomplished by creating gourmet frozen pizzas that exceed the quality of the pizza chain restaurants. Third, company 3 (Gourmet Pizza Company) might try improve its convenience so it moves higher on the y-axis. It could improve convenience by increasing its range of delivery or by adding a second location in another part of the city of Tampa. Then it would be appealing to a larger potential market.

- Which companies are in a position of weakness?

  Any company can use a strategic group map to evaluate it position relative to rivals in the industry. As mentioned above, Gourmet Pizza Company (#3) appears to be in a good position, but Eddie & Sam's (#4) is in a weaker position. Its pizza is about equal in toppings and flavors compared to Cici's Pizza, but Eddie & Sam's is less convenient.

A common criticism of strategic group maps is that they are "too subjective" or they are "based on opinions instead of facts." This is an important issue. In any analysis, the source and quality of the data are important. If the data underlying the analysis are unreliable then the conclusions of the analysis will also be unreliable. Consider the analysis presented in Figure 2.9 – the strategic group map. How was the convenience and the variety of flavors evaluated for each company? If the evaluations were based on the opinion of one person then the map would not be too meaningful. But what if the map was the result of questions answered by 1000 people (in Tampa) who were avid pizza eaters? If so, the map would reflect informed opinions of a large sample of people. And it would be helpful source of information for any competitors in the market. It is true that the map represents the subjective opinions of consumers (on the y-axis), but those opinions are how people make their purchasing decisions. Perception is reality! If consumers believe something is true about a company's products (or its brand) then they will act on those beliefs. The subjective nature of a strategic group map is a strength, if the map is constructed with reliable data. With the growing popularity of data visualization and infographics published on the internet, there are other methods for representing an industry that have become prominent. Many are similar to a strategic group map because they show the "big picture" of how companies in an industry compete with each other.

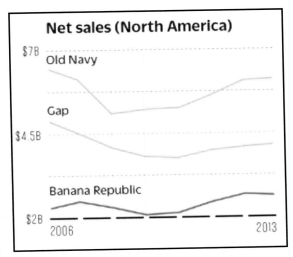

Consider the retail clothing industry. Gap, Inc. had declining sales every year from 2006 to 2011 and has never regained the prominent position it once held. Its other key brands (Old Navy and Banana Republic) have slumped too. The Great Recession was partly to blame, but the brands have not recovered. What happened to such a powerful American brand? Figure 2.10 appeared in in Fast Company (Sacks, 2015) as a way to illustrate how companies in the retail clothing industry have surrounded Gap, Inc. The author concluded that the company's strategy had gotten a little stale – it was still using a business model that was innovative about 30 years ago. New fast-moving competitors like H&M and Zara have set the standard for "fast fashion" and Gap has not responded well. If you believe the author's analysis, all three of Gap's brands are arranged on nearly the same vertical line. All three are positioned right in the middle of the industry, halfway between "trendy" and "classic". Maybe a shift to the left or the right would be a wise shift for one of the brands.

The infographic doesn't show the market share of the companies, but it is still a useful method for showing the strategic diversity in the industry. Other similar infographics that summarize the competitive positioning of companies can be found for the cruise industry (http://tinyurl.com/qd49m6h) and the camera industry (http://tinyurl.com/o79tl25) among many others.

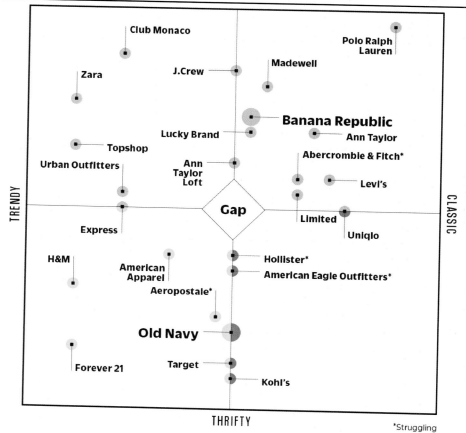

Figure 2.8: Infographic of the Retail Clothing Industry

DRIVING FORCES ANALYSIS

The previous four sections of External Analysis focused on characteristics of the current industry. In this last section of chapter two, we address how and why the industry will change in the future. The way to start with a driving forces analysis is to practice "industry foresight" (Hamel & Prahalad, 1994). Company leaders can easily get distracted by the day-to-day operating decisions that must be made. In contrast, excellent leaders are focused on making strategic decisions (see "Characteristics of Strategic Decisions" in chapter 1) instead of spending all their time on tactical decisions. In fact, *the leader's job is to prepare the organization for the future.* A leader can't prepare for the future by spending all his or her time thinking about the present. To accomplish that task a leader must be alert to important changes in the industry. Hamel & Prahalad (1994) advised leaders that they need to learn how to see the future before their competitors see it.

As a starting point, imagine how your industry will be different 10 years from now. As a specific example, consider a familiar industry: the higher education industry. How will college education be delivered 10 years from now? More on-line courses? More for-profit universities? More interaction among students from different international universities?

Not surprisingly, an accurate ten-year industry foresight is very difficult to create. As an example, imagine if you were the owner of a taxi cab company or a local hotel in the year 2005. If you were developing industry foresight for the future of your industry, would you have identified the telecom industry as a source of threat? Two years later, in June of 2007, the first iPhone was released. Soon after, mobile applications became an entire industry. As of this writing (2019), Uber and Lyft have disrupted the taxi cab industry. A similar but smaller impact has affected the hotel industry because

---

Table 2.3:
The Plastic Shopping Bag "Industry"

- We use 380 billion per year in US.
- Requires 1.6 billion gallons of petroleum oil.
- Cost to manufacture is $.02 - $.04 each
- Only 5.2% are recycled.
- San Francisco spends $8m / year to clean up bags in streets, trees, etc.

Driving Forces analysis:
1. How will this industry be different 10 years from now? Describe it.
2. What will cause these differences to occur between now and then?

Source: Royte (2007).

---

of the house-sharing apps like AirBnB, VRBO, and HomeExchange.com. Both of these examples illustrate that threats and opportunities for an industry can emerge from unlikely sources. Developing industry foresight should be an exercise in creativity that answers the question "what will our industry look like in ten years from now?" For a more comprehensive illustration, see Table 2.3. It describes the details of how Americans use plastic shopping bags. As an exercise in conducting a Driving Forces analysis, read the facts about the industry and answer the two questions. Answering the two questions constitutes the thinking required to conduct a Driving Forces analysis.

After the industry of the future has been described, the next step is to consider *why* the industry will change the way it will. What forces will be driving companies in the industry to make changes? The driving forces are usually divided into four categories: Societal, Technological,

Economic, and Political. In answering question 2 in Table 2.3, there are some obvious economic forces that will change the consumption of plastic bags that are based on the cost of oil. Societal forces will also impact the industry as more Americans begin to value environmentalism.

Every industry experiences change. The purpose of a Driving Forces analysis is to create an intentional alertness to the weak signals that portend change. Some leaders seem to be surprised by change, while others are ready for change – and in fact they see change as an opportunity. By constantly examining Driving Forces for their industry, leaders will be better prepared to lead their companies into a successful future. Many trends can become driving forces in the future. See the generic list of potential driving forces below.

<u>Potential Driving Forces</u>

- Changes in long-term industry growth rate
- Changes in who buys the product and how they use it
- Product innovation
- Technological change/process innovation
- Marketing innovation
- Entry or exit of major firms
- Diffusion of technical knowledge
- Increasing globalisation of industry
- Changes in cost and efficiency
- Market shift from standardized to differentiated products (or vice versa)
- New regulatory policies and/or government legislation
- Changing societal concerns, attitudes, and lifestyles
- Changes in degree of uncertainty and risk

For Further Consideration

Hopefully Chapter 2 has successfully illustrated the importance of studying the traits, forces, competitors, and trends in an industry. In today's technology-enabled and global economy, industries can change quickly and frequently. Maybe a less-appreciated skill for industry analysis is the role of creativity. Did leaders in the taxi cab industry see the threat of Uber and Lyft? Eventually they did, but did they recognize the threat early enough to prepare a successful response? Probably, most of them did not. Sometimes threats and opportunities emerge from unrelated industries - so far afield that they might seem superfluous to a company's future.

Consider the example of the driverless car. In 2019, everyone knows about the concept. Did you know that in 2012, a Google self-driving car travelled more than 300,000 miles without a mishap (Dumain, 2012:31). And, in 2010, four driverless electric vans drove about 8000 miles from Italy to China.

Figure 2.1 – Google's Driverless Car

Widespread adoption of driverless cars is likely to impact many industries besides the automobile industry. What implications can you imagine? What industries might be affected, and what opportunities might be created when driverless cars become common?

https://www.bbc.com/news/technology-19829906

Chapter 2 presented the details of External Analysis, which corresponds to section 2.a) of the Strategy Process Cycle (see Figure 1.2). The five steps of External Analysis are 1) economic conditions of the industry, 2) Five Forces Analysis, 3) Key Success Factors, 4) Strategic Group Analysis, and 5) Driving Forces Analysis. In the next chapter, the book will explain internal analysis, which corresponds to section 2.b) of the Strategy Process Cycle.

Response to "For Further Consideration"

On the previous page, we considered the emergence of driverless cars. The vignette ended with a series of questions. "Widespread adoption of driverless cars is likely to impact many industries besides the automobile industry."
- What implications can you imagine?
- What industries might be affected, and what opportunities might be created when driverless cars become popular?

Four ways self-driving vehicles may change business
1. On highways, trucks could travel 12 inches apart in "platoons" that reduce drag. Fuel savings could reach 15% to 20%.
2. Per year, Americans spend on average 250 hours commuting to and from work. If a car does the driving, that time could be spent working, resting, or socializing.
3. Why are cars made of steel? Because steel provides the best protection of passengers during a collision. Since self-driving cars will be safer, they won't need heavy safety cages. This outcome could be bad news for the steel industry.
4. With fewer collisions, insurance premiums should be lower and insurance claims will be less. But insurance companies will have to figure out who's liable in an accident: the car maker, the software designer, or the GPS provider.

Additional information about the main segments of the entertainment industry. The music segment had been the largest for many years, but beginning in 2006, the gaming industry enjoyed unprecedented growth. Due to advances in internet speeds, graphics quality, and processor speeds, gaming became a very competitive source of entertainment.

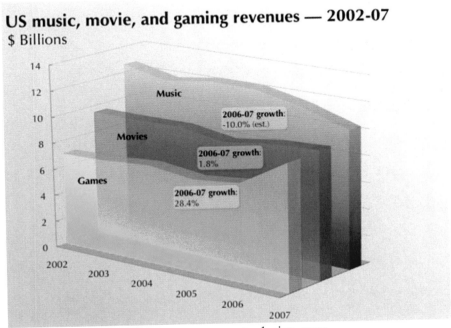

Source: www.arstechnica.com

Chapter 2: Industry & External Analysis

Answers for Review & Discussion

1. Answers:

a) The "threat of new entrants" increases as economies of scale become <u>less important</u>: Economies of scale can be a barrier to entry because strong scale economies often give incumbent companies a cost advantage over new entrants. See Figure 2.5 for a review of economies of scale. In this situation, a new entrant must either enter on a large scale (which requires a large capital investment and can create over-capacity problems) or enter on a small scale but face a cost disadvantage. Either way, a new entrant has a barrier that it must overcome if scale economies are powerful in an industry.

b) The "threat of new entrants" increases as customer loyalty becomes <u>weaker</u>: Strong customer loyalty creates a barrier to entry because it means that customers in an industry are rarely willing to switch providers of the good or service that they are consuming. When potential new entrants realize that customers tend to be brand loyal, they may be discouraged from trying to enter the industry only to struggle to gain market share.

c) The "threat of new entrants" increases as incumbent companies <u>mildly</u> retaliate: When incumbent companies are expected to strongly retaliate against new entrants, this threat makes new entrants more wary of actually entering an industry. On the other hand, if incumbents have a history of ignoring new entrants, then future new entrants are more likely to attempt to gain a foothold in the industry.

d) The "threat of new entrants" increases as customers incur <u>low</u> switching costs: When customers incur low costs to switch from one brand to another, new entrants believe they have a reasonable chance of gaining market share in the industry. In contrast, if customers in the industry tend to be brand loyal, new entrants probably believe they will have a very hard time gaining traction in the industry.

2. Answers:

a) The "power of suppliers" increases as the uniqueness of the supplied input <u>increases</u>: When a supply is rare or unique, the vendor of that supply is likely to become more powerful. This is true because buyers of the supply are usually not able to find it widely available. So the vendors that do have it are able to dictate terms of the sale.

b) The "power of suppliers" increases as the size of suppliers <u>increases</u>: As a general rule, the larger the supplier (in terms of gross annual revenue) the more powerful the supplier will be.

c) The "power of suppliers" increases as the number of suppliers <u>decreases</u>: In cases where the number of suppliers to an industry shrinks, the remaining suppliers are usually more powerful than they were before the contraction. For example, consider a situation where there are five suppliers to an industry. If companies 1 and 2 merge, then companies 3 and 4 merge there will be three companies remaining. On average, those three companies will be more powerful than the five that existed before the mergers.

References

Ars Technica website. http://arstechnica.com/news.ars/post/20080124-growth-of-gaming-in-2007-far-outpaces-movies-music.html . Accessed 9/28/08.

Bloomberg. (2019). Rare Earths Battle Looms as U.S. Aims to Counter China Export Threat. https://www.bloomberg.com/news/articles/2019-06-05/rare-earths-battle-looms-as-u-s-aims-to-counter-china-threat . Accessed 6/6/19.

Bryant, A. (1996). Union Pacific's Plan to Merge Hits Resistance At 3 Agencies. New York Times, Business, p. C1.

Copple, B. 2002. Forbes. Shelf-Determination. Accessed 10/4/08.

De Gorter, H & Just, D. 2008. The Economics of U.S. Ethanol Import Tariffs with a Consumption Mandate and Tax Credit. Unpublished working paper, Cornell University, Department of Applied Economics and Management.

De la Merced, Michael. (2011). AT&T Ends $39 Billion Bid for T-Mobile. New York Times, 12/19/11. Accessed 6/29/13. http://dealbook.nytimes.com/2011/12/19/att-withdraws-39-bid-for-t-mobile/?_r=0

Dumaine, B. (2012). The driverless revolution. *Fortune*. November 12, pp. 31-32.

Hamilton, A. 2008. Why Circuit City Busted, While Best Buy Boomed. Time. Accessed 11/11/08. http://www.time.com/time/business/article/0,8599,1858079,00.html

Federal Trade Commission. 2003. Slotting Allowances in the Retail Grocery Industry: Selected Case Studies in Five Product Categories. Accessed on the FTC website at http://www.ftc.gov/os/2003/11/slottingallowancerpt031114.pdf . Accessed 10/4/08.

Fung, E. (2019). Landlords to Tesla: No easy out on store leases. Wall Street Journal. March 9: p. B1.

Hamel, G. and Prahalad, C.K. 1994. Competing for the Future. Boston: Harvard Business School Press.

Keng, C. (2018). Forbes. https://www.forbes.com/sites/cameronkeng/2018/03/26/why-uber-eats-will-eat-you-into-bankruptcy/#4340496221f6 . Accessed 6/5/19.

McWilliams, D. (1997). Whirlwind on the web. Business Week. Aug 1: 132-136.

Natterman, P. (2000). Best practice ≠ best strategy. McKinsey Quarterly, 2: 22-31.

Porter, M.E. (1980). Competitive Strategy: Techniques for Analyzing Industries and Competitors. New York: The Free Press.

Professional Education Organization International website (www.peoi.org) accessed 10/6/08.

Royte, E. (2007). Moneybags. Fast Company, October. http://www.fastcompany.com/magazine/119/moneybags.html. Accessed 12/15/08.

Sacks, D. (2014). Inside Gap's plan to get back into your drawers. Fast Company, April. http://www.fastcompany.com/3042434/gapquest . Accessed 7/1/15.

Spencer, S. & Kneebone, M. (2007). FoodMap: A comparative analysis of Australian food distribution channels. Australian Government Department of Agriculture, Fisheries and Forestry, Canberra. Accessed 9/21/10. http://www.daff.gov.au/__data/assets/pdf_file/0003/298002/foodmap-full.pdf

Notes for Chapter 2

Chapter 3:
Company & Internal Analysis

<u>Introduction</u>

For the introduction to Chapter 3, turn back to the "Characteristics of Strategic Decisions" in Chapter 1. In that section of the book, you learned that strategic decisions (as opposed to tactical or operating decisions) must "<u>match the activities of the organization to the resources</u> that it controls" (point #3). The purpose of this chapter is to evaluate the resources and capabilities that are under control of the organization. Once a management team has a clear understanding of the resources at its disposal, it can develop an effective strategy based on those resources.

The illustration at the beginning of Chapter 2 described the requirement for a basketball coach to "know the competition" before devising a game plan. Obviously, knowing the competition is only half of the story. An effective coach must also know the strengths and weaknesses of each player, and the strengths and weaknesses of the team. Only then can the coach develop a game plan that capitalizes on the team's strengths, minimizes its weaknesses, and exploits its opportunities. Chapter 3 explains step 2.b) of the Strategy Process Cycle (Figure 1.3).

<u>Learning Objectives for Chapter 3:</u>

1. Demonstrate competence in using financial ratios
2. Conduct a value chain analysis of an organization's business model.
3. Assess an organization's competitive advantage using a VRIO analysis.

Opening Vignette for Chapter 3

One of the largest, most successful, and most innovative privately-held companies in the US is unknown to many people. It employs about 10,000 and has annual revenue of about $3.5 billion. It manufactures products in the medical, aerospace, automotive, and textile industries. If you have ever worn a rain coat or clothing for snow skiing, you have probably benefitted from the company's technology. The company, W.L. Gore & Associates, started in 1958 as a husband and wife team. The first big success was Gore-Tex, a patented waterproofing membrane that was licensed and used by many famous outdoor clothing companies: The North Face, Columbia, and LL Bean, among others. As competitors began to imitate the features of Gore-Tex, the company was prepared to launch an incredible array of new products, seemingly unrelated to its breathable, waterproof fabric. The company makes stents to open human arteries, wiring & cables for NASA spacecraft, guitar strings, and has started developing artificial corneas that will replace diseased ones in people who are waiting for transplant donors (Bennett, 2019)

How can one company make so many products in divergent industries? The answer is that WL Gore owns a few underlying resources that contribute to all its products. The most important is a patent related to a chemical compound that has the familiar name of Teflon. The compound is polytetrafluoroethylene and it forms the basis for almost all of WL Gore's products. Over the years, Gore has developed incredible chemical and engineering expertise in creating new applications for Teflon.

Figure 3.1: Some WL Gore Product Lines

Consumer Products   Filtration   Cables

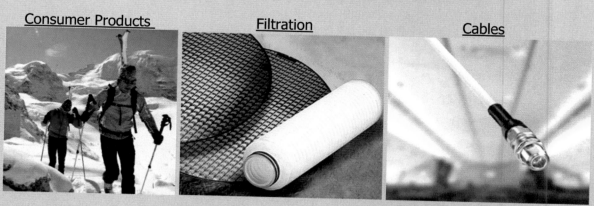

The last section of chapter 3 introduces the concept of the "resource-based" view of the firm. This perspective encourages us to realize that successful companies own valuable and rare resources that are hard for competitors to imitate. Those resources allow a company to develop excellent products and services. The takeway from this example is that a company's competencies and resources are the source of competitive advantage, not its products and services.

FINANCIAL RATIO ANALYSIS

The first step in Internal Analysis is to understand how well the current strategy is performing. If the company is excelling in all the areas that it measures, then there is probably not a need to make drastic alterations to the strategy. If however the organization is not performing well, then managers must take the diagnosis as a sign that corrections must be made. In this chapter we will examine some very rudimentary financial ratios. There are many financial metrics that we will not consider here. Those can be reviewed in a corporate finance textbook. In this author's experience, it is too common that students arrive into a strategy course without a solid understanding of how to assess the basic financial situation of a company. Until a person can make sense of an income statement, balance sheet, and cash flow statement, he or she will struggle to create effective strategy. Also, the ratios presented below will probably be less useful to a non-profit organization. While non-profits do have financial goals managers of non-profits should set financial goals and determine whether the organization is meeting those goals. Examples might address areas such as subscriber revenue growth, total cost per member, or operating cost control. Financial ratios are typically divided into four categories: profitability, liquidity, efficiency, and leverage. Before presenting the formulae for the ratios in each section, a quick review of income statements and balance sheets will be presented.

Income Statement

See Table 3.1 for a summary of a generic income statement. Line 1 represents all the revenue the organization has generated over a fixed time period (one year, one month, one quarter, etc). In fact, all the entries on an income statement measure money earned or spent during a fixed time period. Line 2 is mostly pertinent to an organization that sells or manufactures products (as opposed to services). Cost of goods sold (COGS) is how much money the organization

Table 3.1: Income Statement
1. Total Revenue or Sales
2. Cost of Goods Sold
3. = Gross Profit
4. Operating Expenses
5. = Operating Profit (EBIT)
6. - Interest Expense
7. = Earnings before taxes (EBT)
8. - Income taxes
9. = Net income after taxes (NIAT)

spent when it purchased the parts, materials, suppliers, or products that it eventually resold to customers. Note that this category **does not** include expenses like salaries or rent that are associated with operating the business. Line 3 (gross profit) is the first category of profit that can be measured. Gross profit is the difference between total revenue and cost of goods sold. For retailers, another way to think about gross profit is that it indicates the average markup that the retailer charges. Imagine a retailer that imports rugs from Turkey to the US. If the company buys the rugs for $40 each and sells them for $60 each, the gross profit is $20 ($60 – $40) and the markup is 50% (60-40)/40). Line 4 of the income statement is a catch-all category that includes many expenses. Any expense incurred for the purpose of running the organization is usually counted in the operating expenses. Common examples are rent, salaries, insurance premiums, electricity and other utilities payments, and maintenance. Some non-cash expenses often occur in this category. Specifically, depreciation and amortization are expenses that help account for the value of assets, but they don't require a payment to anyone. After all those expenses are deducted, the result is Line 5, Operating Profit, also known as Earnings before Interest & Taxes (EBIT). Interest expense (line 6) doesn't always appear a separate line item, but sometimes is lumped into operating expenses. Either way, it shows how much the organization spent on interest payments on borrowed money. Of course some companies have not borrowed any money, so they would not have any interest payments. Line 7 indicates the next line of profit, earnings before taxes. Line 8 shows how much income tax the organization must pay for the period, and line 9 is net profit (NIAT).

Balance Sheet

Table 3.2 is a generic balance sheet showing the three categories of accounts: assets, liabilities, and owner's equity. In each area, items are listed in order of liquidity. For example, cash is the most liquid asset so it is listed as the first asset, while property, plant, and equipment is listed last because it is the least liquid. In Europe, the convention is reversed: the top line of the list of assets shows the least liquid asset first. An important feature of any balance sheet is that it must balance, as defined by the fundamental accounting equation "assets = liabilities + equity." While an income statement shows the activity that happened during a set period of time, a balance sheet is a "snapshot" of a company's financial condition at one day in time. For example, if the balance sheet is dated June 30, 2019, it means the company's financial condition is illustrated in the statement on that day. At the end of the next day, July 1, 2019, the company's financial condition might be different. Maybe the company took out a loan and bought some equipment. The new balance sheet would show an increase in debt on the liabilities side and an increase in PP&E on the asset side.

Line 1 measures all the organization's most liquid assets – cash and marketable securities that can be converted into cash quickly. Lines 1-4 on this balance sheet are usually categorized as liquid or

Table 3.2: Balance Sheet

Assets
1. Cash & equivalents
2. Accounts receivable
3. Inventory
4. Prepaid expenses
5. Notes receivable
6. Property, Plant, Equip.
   7. TOTAL ASSETS

Liabilities
8. Accounts payable
9. Current portion of LTD
10. Notes payable
   11. TOTAL LIABILITIES

Owner's Equity
12. Retained earnings
13. Common stock
   14. TOTAL EQUITY

short-term assets. Accounts receivable represents money that is owed to the organization and should be received within 30 days. Usually the money is owed by customers who bought something on credit. In addition to accounts receivable, many balance sheets will also indicate how much money is expected to become uncollectible. Whenever credit is extended to customers, some portion of the payments will never be received. If included, the account is usually called something like "allowance for doubtful accounts". Line 3 is a measure of the value of the entire inventory that the organization owns at the time the balance sheet was written. Inventory is considered a short-term asset, but usually cannot be liquidated (converted into cash) in less than 30 days. Prepaid expenses (line 4) are expenses that have been paid but are not yet due to the vendor. Line 5 and 6 are long-term assets. Notes receivable represents money that is owed to the company – usually from the owners or other borrowers who have borrowed money on a long-term basis, which is different from short-term trade credit. Line 6 (often called PP&E) is the book value of all the long-term assets that the organization owns. On many balance sheets, the accumulated depreciation will also be shown. The book value of the assets minus the accumulated depreciation should be approximately equal to the market value of the assets at the time the balance sheet was written.

On the liabilities side of the balance sheet, accounts are also arranged according to liquidity. Line 8, accounts payable, shows the amount owed to short-term creditors. This amount usually represents trade credit owed to vendors of supplies or inventory. Line 9 shows the portion of long-term debt that is due currently, within the next 30 days. Line 10 is the total long term debt that the organization owes to lenders.

Equity

According to the fundamental accounting equation, equity is simply the difference between total assets and total liabilities. It is usually divided into several components, with retained earnings (line 12) and common stock (line 13) being the most commonly seen. Retained earnings is the accumulated earnings that the company has generated since inception. If a company loses money in a year, retained earnings will decrease. Remember that retained earnings is an accounting concept used for making a balance sheet actually balance, so it is not money that the company has available to spend or invest. Common stock is the value of the ownership in the company. In a publicly traded company the common stock is owned by thousands or even millions of shareholders. A small privately held company can issue stock to its founders and other owners.

After this brief review of the basic components of the two main financial statement, we can present a review of basic financial ratios. (Note: a third common statement is the statement of cash flows, which we did not review here).

Profitability ratios illustrate the organization's ability to generate profits from the revenue that it earns. There are different kinds of profitability, based on the point in the income statement where the profitability is measured (see Table 3.1).

$$1. \text{ Gross Profit Margin} = \frac{\text{Gross Profit}}{\text{Total Revenue}}$$

GPM is the profit margin the company earns over the price it paid for its inventory and raw materials. It applies to organizations that sell a product but not service companies. For example, restaurants are careful to monitor their GPM. If the cost of materials rises (e.g. ingredients for recipes) then GPM will fall unless the restaurant can raise its menu prices to compensate for higher ingredients costs. In April 2019, President Trump threatened to close the border between the US and Mexico as a response to the flow of illegal immigration. The threat promised to stop people from crossing the border, but also goods and services. About 75% of US consumption is from avocados imported from Mexico. In response to the threat, prices jumped 34% on April 3 and Chipotle announced it would increase the prices of its burritos to compensate for higher food costs (Hertzer, 2019). The most common way to interpret any profit margin is as a percent. So if gross profit is $40,000 and total revenue is $90,000, then gross profit margin is 44.4%. For each $1.00 in revenue the organization generates, it retains 44¢ in gross profit.

$$2. \ \text{Operating Profit Margin} = \frac{\text{EBIT}}{\text{Total Revenue}}$$

OPM is the profit margin earned from normal operations of the organization. Operating profit (aka EBIT) shows how much income the organization has available to pay its interest expenses (line 6 of Table 3.1) and taxes Operating Margin is important to measure because it helps determine whether operating expenses (line 4, Table 3.1) are being managed well. Operating expenses is usually a broad category that includes wages, rent or mortgage payments, insurance, utilities, travel costs, professional fees, administrative fees, and other costs that are required to maintain the organization's operations. If a manager examines profit margin trends, and discovers that gross profit is stable but operating margin is falling, what conclusion should he make? See the answer at the end of this section.

$$3. \ \text{Net Profit Margin} = \frac{\text{NIAT}}{\text{Total Revenue}}$$

NPM is the "bottom line" profit margin. It shows how much income is available as a percentage of total revenue and is the most common measure of overall profitability of the organization. At this point in the income statement (line 9 of Table 3.1) all expenses have been paid - including income taxes - and the net profit is money the company can retain or reinvest into its future.

$$4. \ \text{Return on Assets} = \frac{\text{NIAT}}{\text{Total Assets}}$$

Return on Assets (also known as return on investment or ROI) compares net income in the numerator to Total Assets in the denominator. It shows how much the company earns per each dollar it has invested in assets. This concept is important because at the end of the day, the reason that an organization buys assets is ultimately to generate sales. If assets do not help create revenue, then a manager could question why they were purchased.

Answer to OPM question: if gross margin (GPM) is stable but operating margin (OPM) is falling, it probably indicates that the manager is doing a good job managing the cost of goods sold, but the operating expenses are rising too fast. He should check some specific expenses like utilities, or wages, or insurance premiums to find the account that is too high.

Liquidity ratios demonstrate whether the organization has sufficient liquidity, which is defined as the ability to meet short term financial obligations (those that are due within 30 days). An organization might have plenty of long term assets and capital, but not enough cash to pay the bills that will be due soon.

$$5. \ \text{Current ratio} = \frac{\text{Current assets}}{\text{Current liabilities}}$$

The current ratio compares the current assets on the balance sheet to the current liabilities. At a minimum, the ratio should be above 1.0 (i.e. current assets are greater than current liabilities). In most industries, a ratio of 2.0 or above is considered a good target as a rule of thumb.

$$6. \ \text{Quick ratio} = \frac{\text{Current assets - inventory}}{\text{Current liabilities}}$$

The quick ratio is also known as the "acid test" ratio because it is a more stringent test of liquidity. Among all the current assets, inventory is the least liquid. It usually consists of finished goods or goods in process that cannot be sold (and converted to cash) very quickly. So the truest test of liquidity is to consider current assets without the inventory included. In some industries, inventory is especially illiquid. A car dealerships usually has millions of dollars of inventory on the balance sheet, but it can't expect to convert that inventory into sales quickly. In contrast, a grocery store has a lot of perishable inventory (fresh food). That kind of inventory must be sold quickly or it loses all its value and must be written off as a loss.

Activity ratios assess whether the company is running its operations efficiently, or how well its resources are being deployed. They are important for all organizations, not just those that are trying to compete using a low cost or low price strategy. As an organization becomes more efficient, it will usually become more competitive too.

$$7. \text{ Asset Turnover ratio} = \frac{\text{Total Revenue}}{\text{Total Assets}}$$

There is one main reason that organizations buy assets: to help the organization generate more sales. When assets are purchased that do not help generate more revenue, a person might question whether the purchase was wise. A good question to evaluate the wisdom of purchasing an asset: "When we own this asset, will it help us generate more revenue?" For example, when a university spends lots of money on landscaping its campus with expensive palm trees, do those assets generate a return? Maybe a beautiful campus helps convince prospective students to enroll in the future, and retain existing students to continue their education. This question is slightly over-simplified, but it does give a good criteria for evaluating whether a purchase is a smart one. Some assets might never help generate revenue (maybe they help reduce costs instead). The asset turnover ratio illustrates the degree to which assets are generating revenue. If the asset turnover ratio is 0.83 we can say that the organization generates $.83 in revenue for each dollar in assets that it owns. If the asset turnover is increasing over time, it indicates that the organization is creating more sales from that same dollar invested in assets.

$$8. \text{ Inventory Turnover ratio} = \frac{\text{Cost of Goods Sold}}{\text{Inventory}}$$

Inventory turnover describes how quickly an organization is able to convert (turn) its inventory into sales. If inventory sits on the shelves for a long time, the ratio will be low but if inventory arrives into the organization and sells quickly, the ratio will be large. The label for this ratio is "number of times per year," so if the result is 4.6 times, it indicates that the organization sells out its entire inventory 4.6 times during the year. This ratio is only applicable to organizations that stock and sell products rather than service based organizations. Restaurants and retailers are especially interested in their inventory turnover ratio.

$$9. \text{ Avg. Collection Period} = \frac{\text{Accounts Receivable}}{(\text{Sales} / 360)}$$

Average collection period measures the approximate time it takes an organization to collect payments for the sales it makes on credit. Many organizations have very small credit sales, so this ratio would not apply to those situations. For organizations that do sell goods or services on trade credit (usually to other companies instead of consumers) this ratio is a good way to track whether customers are paying their bills on time. The result of the ratio is labeled in days, so if the answer is 25 days, it indicates that it takes an average of 25 days for the organization to convert its credit sales in to cash. If terms of a credit sale require payment in 20 days, an average collection of 25 days shows that the company's customers are taking too long to pay their bills.

Leverage ratios are useful for examining the capital structure of an organization. Specifically, these ratios illustrate the relative balance between debt and equity that the organization has employed to finance its operations. Figure 3.2 illustrates capital structure as a combination of debt + equity. When the debt piece becomes very large compared to the equity piece, we say that the company has high leverage. Understanding the balance between the two is important because more debt on the balance sheet creates a riskier capital structure. Students without a firm understanding of corporate finance often miss

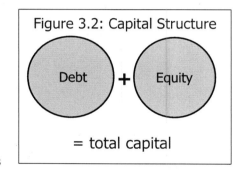

this fact. Why is a highly leveraged balance sheet considered risky? When a company uses leverage (e.g. a loan from a bank), it creates a legal obligation to meet certain goals and repay interest and principle on a schedule. For example, borrowing money from a bank usually requires a company to agree to "loan covenants" which can restrict the decisions that managers in the company can make. A loan covenant might prohibit the purchase of expensive assets without the bank's permission, or require the company to maintain certain cash flow or profitability targets.

Using debt to finance growth is effective because it allows the firm to grow faster than it could using only funds that it generates internally. So the use of debt is named "leverage" because it allows the firm to accomplish more work with the same investment. In physics, leverage allows a person to lift more mass with the same amount of force, just as financial leverage allows the firm to grow faster than it could without leverage.

$$10. \quad \text{Debt Ratio} = \frac{\text{Total Liabilities}}{\text{Total Assets}}$$

The debt ratio is the broadest measure of an organization's leverage. It does not distinguish between short and long term liabilities, but compares all liabilities in the numerator to all assets in the denominator. If the ratio is greater than 1.0 it means that the firm has more liabilities than assets (i.e. it owes more than it owns). In such a situation, the firm would be threatened if lenders began to make demands that loans be repaid.

$$11. \quad \text{Debt to Equity} = \frac{\text{Total Liabilities}}{\text{Total Equity}}$$

The debt to equity ratio (#11) is similar to the debt ratio (#10). It compares the amount of debt on the balance sheet to the amount of equity. And since equity = assets – liabilities, (see line #14 in Table 3.2) this ratio compares how much money is owed to creditors versus the market value of the owners' investment in the company.

$$12. \quad \text{Times Interest Earned} = \frac{\text{Operating Income}}{\text{Interest Expense}}$$

Times interest earned is the only leverage ratio that uses items from the income statement instead of the balance sheet. It compares line 5 of Exhibit 3.1 to line 6 to indicate whether the organization has generated sufficient income to pay its interest expense. Ideally the ratio would be 2.0 or greater, meaning that the organization has earned twice as much income as it must pay to its creditors.

Interpreting Financial Ratios

For the purpose of internal analysis and understanding the results of a company's strategy, an analyst should calculate financial ratios and then make three sets of comparisons to interpret the ratios.

First, the ratios can be compared to industry averages or the ratios of key competitors. Comparison data can be found in publications by Robert Morris & Associates, Moody's, or Standard & Poor. Most universities subscribe to one or more of these data collection & analysis services. Figure 3.3 shows data collected by Standard & Poor's service called "NetAdvantage". It shows the Inventory Turnover ratio of all the publicly traded companies in the retail and specialty retail industries (Yanushevsky, 2019, p. 7). For a person analyzing or managing a retail company, knowing the industry-wide trends in inventory turnover is a useful

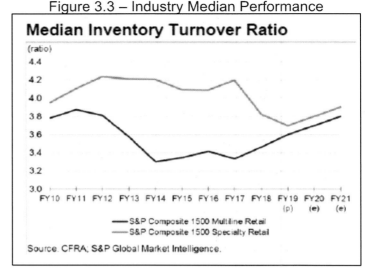

Figure 3.3 – Industry Median Performance

piece of information. These publications collect data from a cross-section of companies in an industry, and then publish average ratios for the industry, keeping the individual company results anonymous. These publications can be useful for benchmarking a company's financial ratios against other companies in the same industry.

A second way to interpret financial ratios is to compare them to history, or to create a trend line. If a company's ROA is better than the industry average, but is declining compared to previous years, there may be cause for alarm.

Third, a manager can use financial ratios to set goals for the organization. Then at the end of the period, the actual results can be compared to the goals to determine which goals were accomplished. For example, in his letter to shareholders in the 2007 *Annual Report*, the CEO of Panera Bread Company wrote "we must focus on growing gross profit per transaction year-over-year" (Shaich, 2008). So, one goal at Panera Bread Company for 2008 is for gross profit margins to be higher than in 2007.

Of course financial ratios are not the only way for a manager to evaluate an organization's performance. Most organizations set some goals that are not measured with financial ratios. For example, in an R&D intensive company, obtaining research grants or creating patents might be important measures of performance. In other courses, students might learn about techniques such as the Balance Scorecard approach (Kaplan & Norton, 1996), Just in Time inventory control, or

Total Quality Management. In any case, financial ratios are only one method of measuring performance. After the recent performance of the organization is understood, the next step in Internal Analysis is to evaluate the organization's activities and resources.

Finally, it is important to remember that financial ratios should not be examined in isolation. They can divulge important trends in how well a company's strategy is working, but they don't tell the whole story. A company could have excellent financial ratios, but at the same time, it could have declining revenue. A thorough analyst must consider the ratios and the dollars!

VALUE CHAIN ANALYSIS

The second step in Internal Analysis is to evaluate the organization's value chain. The value chain is a chronological depiction of all the activities an organization uses to produce its products and services. It shows the linked set of activities the organization performs in order to generate profit. Ideally, each activity that an organization performs will add some value to the final product or service. If an activity exists (and creates costs) but does not create obvious value, a manager might question whether the activity should be discontinued. A more common synonym might be "business model". Anytime we produce a model of something, the model is a simplification of reality. The value chain or business model of a company is merely a simplified explanation (i.e. drawing) of its strategy.

Before discussing the value chain model, what does it mean for an activity to "create" or "add" value? Value creation is more of a philosophy than a measurable concept, but a helpful visual aid is presented in Figure 3.4. The rectangle is composed of three sections, labeled C (cost), P-C (profit), and V-P (consumer surplus). Starting from the bottom, cost is measured from the company's perspective. It contains all the costs the company incurs to bring its product or service to market. The next region is profit (P-C), which is simply the

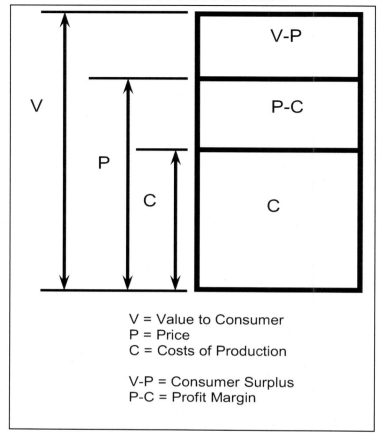

Figure 3.4
Illustration of Value Creation

V = Value to Consumer
P = Price
C = Costs of Production

V-P = Consumer Surplus
P-C = Profit Margin

company's total revenue minus the total costs. This region can be small or large (or even negative) depending on the company's cost structure and what price the market will pay for its product or service. The top region in the rectangle represents consumer surplus (V-P). It indicates how much value the consumer receives by engaging in a transaction with the company. So this region represents a concept from the consumer's perspective, not the company's perspective. It is hard to assign a precise dollar value to V, so the area of the rectangle (V-P) is probably not measurable in dollars and cents, but it is a concept that will be familiar to most people who have been happy with a purchase they made. At this point, a personal example might be helpful. As consumers, we probably have all discovered a product or service that creates a lot of value for us. Think of something you buy regularly. Now try to estimate how much more you would be willing to pay for the item. If the price were to rise by 10% would you continue to buy it? What if the price were to rise by 20%? (This example should remind you of a concept from your microeconomics course: price elasticity of demand…you might continue to buy the same quantity of the item, even if the price increases). If you are really satisfied with a product or service, and buy it regularly, then your consumer surplus (V-P) is positive. The vendor company has created value for you. If the price were to rise without the value (V) increasing, then your consumer surplus would shrink. At some point the area of the (V-P) rectangle could become so small that you are unwilling to buy the product or service any longer.

Each step in a company's value chain does not sell products or services to consumers. Nevertheless, employees in each department or activity in a company can use the concept of value creation to help improve their effectiveness in contributing to the company's overall strategy. For instance, the Internal Auditing department does not sell services to other departments within a company, but auditors can still take the mindset that their goal should be to create value for the internal customers that they serve. In companies where the corporate culture encourages departments to serve and help each other (rather than "winning" against each other) the understanding of value creation is usually well established.

Figure 3.5 shows the generic value chain model, originally developed by Porter (1980). Several details are important to explain the model. First, the activities in the top row are called *Primary Activities*, because they are the ones that create revenue and profit for an organization. The activities in the bottom row are called *Support Activities* because their role is to create the systems in the company that create the infrastructure for the Primary Activities to perform their roles. Second, this generic value chain might not accurately represent the activities in a company with which you are familiar. For example, some companies do not have any activities in the category of inbound logistics or outbound logistics. They either outsource those activities to other companies, or simply do not need those activities to pursue the strategy that they have devised. One of Porter's main points when discussing the value chain is that good strategy requires making choices about what activities to pursue, but also about what activities not to pursue. This generic value chain in Figure 3.5 fits some, but not all companies. Third, the purpose of a value chain analysis is to draw the value chain of a company, then examine the strength of each activity individually, and then examine the strength of the relationship *between* the activities. Remember, each activity should create value for its customer(s) and each activity should form a strong link with the activities that precede and follow it. You've probably heard the phrase "a chain is only as strong as its weakest link." If a company has a weak activity or weak link in its value chain, the performance of the whole company will be reduced.

Figure 3.5 – The Generic Value Chain

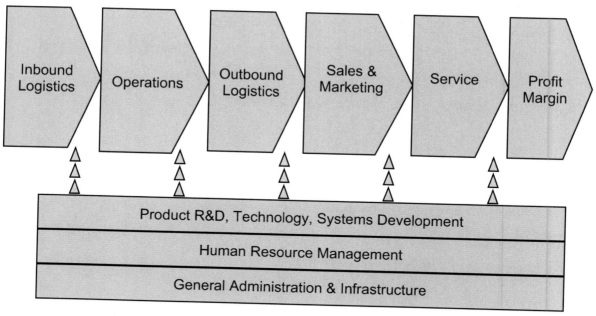

Primary Activities

Inbound Logistics includes all the activities that help acquire the supplies and inputs that the organization needs to conduct its operations. In addition to acquiring the inputs, inbound logistics includes storing and managing the inventory of the inputs. In organizations that buy and handle inputs that are bulky, expensive, or perishable, this activity can be a critical and expensive activity. For any business that is based on products, Inbound Logistics is clearly a key activity. For a restaurant, this activity includes identifying food wholesalers and distributors for all its ingredients. Some perishable ingredients must be delivered daily; other items can be delivered much less frequently. Whoever is responsible for buying food must also manage costs because food makes up a large part of the total cost structure of a restaurant. If cost of ingredients increases, the restaurant will need to raise menu prices or suffer lower gross profit margins. If the restaurant serves alcohol, separate relationships with those vendors must be managed. Restaurant equipment must be repaired and occasionally replaced. Other supplies like uniforms, tableware, furniture, and linens must be purchased and maintained too.

Operations is probably the most encompassing of the Primary Activities. Everything that helps transform inputs into outputs falls into the Operations activity. For most organizations, operations is the heart of what creates the most value for the end user. Using the restaurant example from the previous paragraph, operations begins with menu planning and design, recipe selection, and concludes with food preparation. Delivering the food and presenting it to the customer would occur in the next activity in the value chain. For a manufacturing company, operations is much more involved than for a restaurant. For example, transforming circuit boards, electronic components, glass, and plastic into a television is a much more expensive and complicated process than transforming food into a restaurant meal.

Outbound Logistics occurs as the output from operations is delivered or transferred to the next customer in the chain of activities. As with the first two activities, the composition of this activity varies widely from industry to industry and even from company to company within the same industry. In some industries outbound logistics requires an output to be delivered only a short distance over a short period of time. The restaurant industry is a good example of this situation. Food is delivered to a customer across a counter, or by a waiter who carries the food to a table. Many restaurants have home delivery service, so outbound logistics is a little more complicated. Other industries manage outbound logistics that includes shipping across vast distances using several modes of transportation. In these situations, there is often the requirement that finished goods be warehoused before they are shipped. If the goods are delicate, sensitive, highly valuable, heavy, dangerous, or perishable, other complications must be integrated into the logistics process. Consequently, some companies have elected to outsource this entire activity of the value chain. For example, most consumers consider United Parcel Service (UPS) to be a shipping company. But it also provides a "Distribution Services Network" that can fulfill the entire outbound logistics activity for a company. The UPS website offers this description: "Let UPS Supply Chain Solutions tackle your difficult distribution challenges—working with carriers, managing facilities, handling inventory control, fulfilling orders, and more—so that you can focus on growing your business and gaining new customers."

Sales & Marketing includes the activities the organization uses for receiving and sending information about all its markets. The organization receives (i.e. gathers) information to understand the demands of the customer and the trends in the industry. This process is usually called marketing research and involved collection of primary and secondary data to gather intelligence about customers, competitors, economic features, and demographic trends, among other topics. Second, this activity includes sending information by educating customers about the benefits of the company's outputs and persuading customers to buy them. Sending information to the market using several different communication mediums helps the organization establish its reputation.

Service includes all the activities the organization takes to make customers happy with the transaction, to correct any mistakes in the product or service, and to build a relationship with the customer that generates repeat business. Service can be a simple act like mailing a birthday card to a customer, or as complex as implementing a worldwide recall on a defective product. Anything an organization does to follow-up with a customer after a sale fits into the service category.

Profit Margin is not an activity, but rather is the result when an organization concentrates on creating value at each stage in the value chain.

Support Activities

All the support activities occur throughout the chronology of the value chain. They generate costs, but don't directly generate revenue. Instead of occurring as discrete activities, they support the primary activities continuously. These activities are just as important as the primary activities, and can even be the reason that an organization develops an advantage in its market. For example 3M and Rubbermaid are two companies that have reputations for excellence in research and development. They continually develop innovative products that provide good profit margins and create value for their customers. Human Resource Management (HRM) can also distinguish one company from another. In a published interview, CK Prahalad discussed the importance of HRM.

> the Chinese company that makes the iPod is putting a lot of energy into plant management, and that is an important HR skill. How do you take farm boys and create Six Sigma quality in four years? That question is not trivial. We haven't done it in the US after 20 years. Everybody complains about the Chinese: "These guys are cheap" and I say "Yeah, maybe they're cheap, but they all produce Six Sigma. Why don't you? Indian IT professionals might be cheap, but they are producing Six Sigma quality. Why don't you?" People in China and India recognize the strategic importance of HR, partly because of the tremendous competition for talent. (Kinni, et al, 2008: 133).

<u>Using the Value Chain</u>

So far, we have only discussed definitions and examples of Primary and Support activities in the value chain. But the value chain can be used to understand an organization's strategy and diagnose problems in the organization. To conduct a value chain analysis, follow these steps.

❶ **Draw the organization's current value chain**

The generic value chain in Figure 3.5 is *generic* because it illustrates the business model of some product-based organizations. But to be useful, a value chain diagram should first be drawn to represent the true activities that an organization pursues. It <u>might</u> look a lot like Figure 3.5 but it will probably be quite different. Because a value chain diagram depicts the organization's strategy, it should uniquely express how the organization's activities are arranged. For an example of Dell's value chain, see Figure 3.6. When Michael Dell founded his company in 1984, he created a value chain that was revolutionary compared to the typical PC manufacturers of the time (Compaq and IBM).

Figure 3.6 – Value Chain of Dell Computer Corporation in 1984

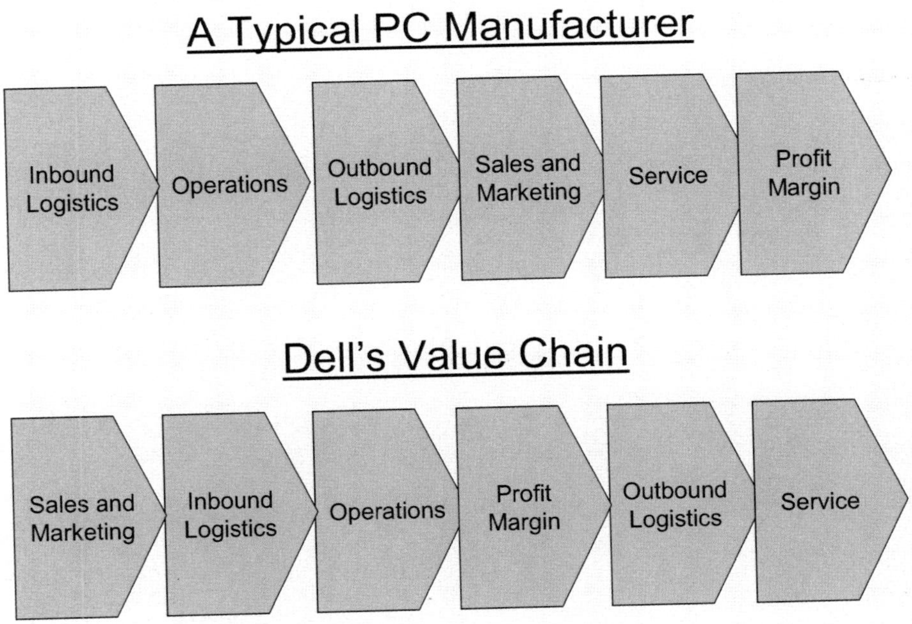

A Typical PC Manufacturer

| Inbound Logistics | Operations | Outbound Logistics | Sales and Marketing | Service | Profit Margin |

Dell's Value Chain

| Sales and Marketing | Inbound Logistics | Operations | Profit Margin | Outbound Logistics | Service |

Notice that the typical PC manufacturer adheres to the generic value chain from Figure 3.5. Now examine the bottom part of Figure 3.6 that illustrates the value chain innovation the Dell created.

Instead of inbound logistics, the first activity is sales & marketing. Since its beginning, Dell has sold the idea of a PC first (and collected money from the customer). Next, Dell buys and receives the parts for the computers that have been ordered (inbound logistics), then Dell builds the PC according to the customer's specifications. At this point in the value chain (end of the 3rd activity), Dell has already determined its profit margin. There may be some small cost in the outbound logistics, but customers typically pay for the shipping costs, so most of Dell's gross profit is known after the operations are completed. In the early days of Dell's history there was very little service after the sale. Today, service represents an important activity for the company.

By comparing the two value chains in Figure 3.6, we can identify several advantages of Dell's model. First, customers are able to customize the PC for themselves. In the old model, customers would buy their PCs from a retailer that usually had only a few configurations available. Dell's mail-order distribution was a little slower than a customer going to a local retailer, but Dell provided a PC configured exactly how the customer wanted it. Second, Dell was the first PC maker to get customers' payments before buying the components that went into the PC. At the time Dell started his company, Compaq and IBM would build a computer and sell it to a retailer, then wait for the retailer to pay the invoice. Dell's innovation made a great improvement in the cash flow of his business compared to his competitors. Third, Dell had almost no inventory costs. Maybe he didn't know it at the time, but Michael Dell designed his company to exploit the most important Key Success Factor (KSF) of his industry. See chapter 2 for a review of the KSF concept. Keeping low inventory levels is more important in this industry than almost any other. Why? Because of rapid product obsolescence. The components for PCs are constantly being improved, faster than many other industries. When a manufacturer buys components and keeps them in inventory until they are installed into a PC, then ships the PC to a retailer, the finished product might be outdated by the time a customer considered buying it.

Step 1 of the value chain analysis requires an intimate knowledge of the company's activities and some creativity to summarize the whole strategy. Almost everyone knows something about Nike – it's one of the most recognizable brands in the world. In its early days, Nike produced only athletic shoes but has since diversified into a number of different sporting goods. Focusing only on the athletic shoes, what would the value chain of Nike look like? See Figure 3.7. The shaded boxes are the only activities that Nike owns and manages inside the company. Starting on the left side, Nike designs and develops products, but it doesn't create its own raw materials – they are purchased from vendors. Next, Nike does not manufacture anything. All the manufacturing is contracted out to companies in low wage countries. Nike gives the specifications to the contractors to make the shoes, but Nike doesn't have the in-house capabilities to manufacture shoes, so manufacturing is not in Nike's value chain. In the 3rd step, Nike does its own marketing (but probably hires some help here too). In the sales & marketing part of the value chain, Nike has some retail stores, but many of its shoes are also sold in other places such as Foot Locker, Academy Sports, and Zappo's. Among all the activities that occur in the athletic shoe industry, Nike really only participates in three: product design, marketing, and retailing. This is a very successful company that has a very simple value chain – the company has chosen to become excellent at a small number of activities and outsource all the others (Crain & Abraham, 2008).

Figure 3.7: Simplified Value Chain of Nike's Athletic Shoe Business

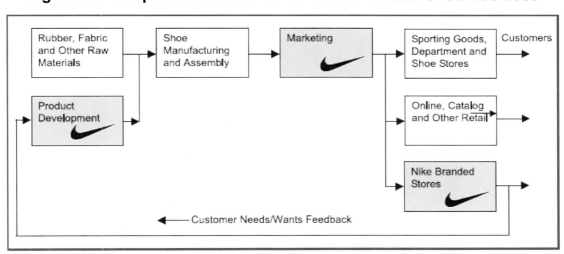

In summary, step 1 of a value chain analysis should be to draw an accurate model of the organization's current value chain. It will probably look very different from the generic value chain in Figure 3.5 and it might look very different from competitors in the same industry. Use some imagination and creativity to draw a value chain. The model should show a simplified picture of the company's business model. It should include the critical steps, actions, or behaviors that the company has designed to deliver its products or services.

The original value chain fits well with a product-base business. For a service business, a step-by-step chronological sequence is less obvious. In later work, Porter introduced the idea of a "value net" which is another way to model a company's strategy. It shows the linked set of activities but emphasizes how they fit together instead of showing a chronological sequence from left to right.

Figure 3.8 shows a value net for the strategy of Southwest Airlines when the company was founded in 1967. Instead of labels like "inbound logistics" and "operations" this model of a strategy identifies the few critical activities that the company pursues, and shows how the activities reinforce each other. For example, Southwest was the first airline to <u>not</u> serve in-flight meals and <u>not</u> use travel agents to book flights for customers. Why? Because the company intentionally decided to offer flights with reduced or limited customer service. Today, this seems normal, but in

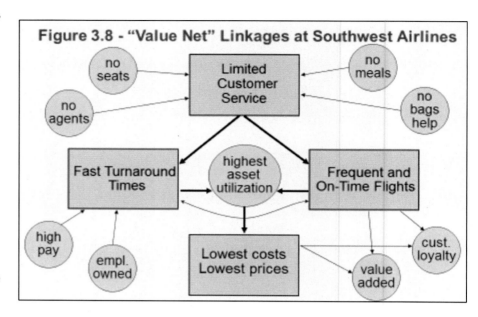

Figure 3.8 - "Value Net" Linkages at Southwest Airlines

1967, air travel was a luxury, and the typical target market was upper middle class consumers. Southwest wanted to limit the level of service so that it could turn planes around faster, and maximize the use of its fleet of aircraft. The company chose asset utilization as its primary goal, so the value net shows how the strategic choices the company made are arranged to support that goal.

❷ **Examine the strength of the linkages between the activities**

Step 1 focuses on the activities in the value chain, and step 2 focuses on the alignment between the activities. Even if the individual activities in the value chain are performed well, the whole organization will not perform well if the activities are not coordinated. There are no pre-established criteria on how to evaluate the linkages between the primary activities. The management team conducting a value chain analysis must decide what criteria are important for evaluating the <u>alignment</u> between activities. For instance, consider the relationship between the primary activities of Sales and Service in Figure 3.5. One way to evaluate the alignment between the two activities might be to test whether customers are hearing similar messages from employees in both activities. If a salesman encourages a customer to have very high expectations then the service activity will bear the brunt of the customer's disappointment if the product does not meet expectations. The employees in the service department face a dilemma in responding to the disappointed customer.

Their response can be something like "we promised you too much – the product was never designed to perform at such high standards" or "sorry the product is defective – would you like a refund or a replacement?" A modern example of broken promises has occurred with the Boeing 787 Dreamliner aircraft. In 2004 All Nippon Airways (2nd largest carrier in Japan) placed an order for 50 planes. Boeing forecasted that the planes would be available about 3½ years later, for delivery in May of 2008. Due to a number of problems, Boeing announced a series of delays. The first planes were finally delivered in September of 2011, about 3½ years behind schedule. In response to the repeated delays, several carriers (Air New Zealand, Virgin Atlantic, Qantas, Air India) have demanded compensation from Boeing because their plans for expansion have been disrupted by Boeing's delayed delivery schedule.

Figure 3.9 – Construction of the Boeing 787 Dreamliner

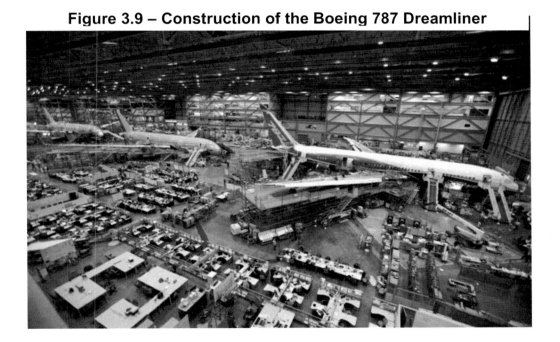

The second step of value chain analysis should reveal relationships between activities that can be streamlined, smoothed, tightened, coordinated, or rearranged. Weaknesses might be evident from poor communication, broken promises, misunderstandings, and delays in throughput. Are the activities tightly aligned and able to reinforce each other? There is a reason Southwest Airlines decided to use open seating instead of assigned seating: it believes open seating is the fastest way to get passengers into the plane, which ultimately helps achieve the goal of having fast turnaround times at the airport.

❸ The third step of value chain analysis is to examine relationships that exist at the beginning and end of the firm's value chain. Just as managers should strive to improve the linkages in the chain within the organization, improvements can also be made in the linkages outside the organization. Most commonly, these improvements come in the form of improved relationships with vendors, joint venture / alliance partners, or customers. A familiar example is when a company establishes electronic data interchange (EDI) with a vendor. The organization might even give limited access to its inventory system so that when inventory becomes low, the vendor will recognize the need to re-stock, then ship the inventory, then send an electronic invoice. Automated communication like this example is faster, more accurate, and cheaper than using a manual system to re-order inventory from a vendor. Traditionally, relationships with customers and vendors tend to be competitive, and sometimes even adversarial. Instead, some companies have viewed these relationships as opportunities to gain advantages that create value for both parties. Preiss, Goldman, and Nagel (1996:1) pioneered this concept by recommending that managers "operate your business as an "interprise"—forming closer, more interactive relationships with customers, suppliers, and even competitors." In the long run, these cooperative relationships help both parties to achieve higher goal attainment.

VRIO ANALYSIS

The third component of conducting a thorough internal analysis is commonly referred to as a VRIO Analysis. As an analogy, it can be considered as a "new & improved" SWOT analysis. Why does SWOT need to be improved? The main problem with the old familiar SWOT analysis is that there are not clear criteria for how to identify a strength, weakness, opportunity, and threat. Specifically, how strong does a strength need to be for it to qualify as a strength? How do we test whether a strength is truly a strength? Must it be in the top 10% of all competitors' strengths? Must it be unique in its industry? Similar questions can be asked about the method for identifying weaknesses, threats, and opportunities.

A VRIO Analysis is based on the "resource-based view" of the firm, originally developed by Jay Barney (1995). The resource-based view (RBV) provides a unique way to understand how companies attain competitive advantage. Typically, managers have viewed their organizations as producers of products or services. We might call this a "product-based view" of an organization. Taking this view, a manager would believe that his company's products and services are the reason it is successful. For example, a barista at Starbuck's might say "we have a competitive advantage because our coffee and other menu items are the best in the industry." In contrast, the RBV suggests that a firm's success is ultimately attributed to the ownership of key resources, not because of the firm's products or services. In most instances, products and services can be copied or substituted, so they cannot be the source of a sustained competitive advantage. By examining a firm's resources (instead of its products), we can determine whether it can achieve a sustained competitive advantage.

Consider the analogy of a citrus tree at peak season. Seen from a distance, the bright yellow or orange fruit can easily become the focus of our attention. If we were to "analyze" the citrus tree, our goal might be to understand why it has become successful. Does the fruit *cause* the tree to be successful? No – the fruit is the outcome of a healthy tree, much like a successful product or service is the outcome of a healthy company. The tree is successful because it has a healthy root system that gives it stability, nutrition, water, and resiliency. We can't see the root system but we know it plays a critical role in the tree's success. In

the same way, the RBV tells us to examine the deeper parts of a company that might be harder to see. Instead of focusing on the products or services (which are easy to see), we should examine the resources that a company owns or controls. A company's resources explain whether and why it is successful. Resources can be broadly defined as anything the firm owns or controls, and are usually identified in four categories: financial, physical, human, and organizational.

To conduct a "VRIO Analysis" the first task is to identify the key resources that the firm owns or controls. At this point, the temptation is to choose the existing strengths or the company. Instead, focus on the resources that are foundational to the company's strategy. These are usually determined partially by the industry norms and partially by the choices that the firm's leaders have made. For most retailers, "location" is a key resource. Being easily accessible to customers is foundational to a retailer's strategy. But in the case of Amazon, location is not a key resource – Amazon has chosen not to compete on the basis of physical location. For McDonald's, location is a foundational resource. In fact, much of the financial and strategic success of McDonald's is attributed not to its products (French fries and hamburgers) but the ownership of prime real estate locations all over the world. In the late 1950s McDonald's created the Franchise Realty Corporation to buy, sell, and manage the company's real estate portfolio (Love, 1987). Franchisees do most the cooking and serving fast food, while the corporation earns money on franchise fees and real estate transactions. Regardless of a company's industry or strategy, it has resources as the foundation of its strategy. The first task in this section is to identify those resources so they can be evaluated according to VRIO, which is explained as the next task. To be practical, it is wise to identify one or two resources from each category: financial, physical, organizational, and human.

The second task of a VRIO analysis is to evaluate the firm's foundational resources. Barney (1995) identified four criteria for determining whether a firm's resources can lead to a sustained competitive advantage. The following sections describe the criteria. About each of the resources, a manager should ask the following questions: are the resources valuable, rare, difficult for competitors to imitate, and are the exploited by the organization? The following sections elaborate on each criterion in a VRIO analysis.

❶ *Are the firm's resources valuable?*

The first criteria in a VRIO Analysis is defined in an unexpected way. Here, "valuable" does not mean the resource is expensive or worth a lot of money. Instead, for a resource to be considered valuable, it must be useful in helping the firm respond to unexpected events. At important points in a firm's history, the valuable resources are the ones that explain why the firm was able to respond with flexibility and innovation. Specifically, valuable resources are those that have helped the firm *overcome threats* or *exploit opportunities*. To consider this criterion, a manager should look for historical evidence that the firm has faced situations when it was able to respond to these unexpected events. One example of exploiting an opportunity was illustrated by Kodak in the late 1800s. It was the first company to create photographic film on a roll (instead of each exposure being captured on a single sheet of film). In 1894 Thomas Edison gave the world's first commercial exhibition of a motion picture in New York City. His camera, called a "kinetoscope," required film that would capture multiple images quickly, and play them back at high speeds (See Figure 3.10). At that time, Kodak was the only company that could provide film in that format. Kodak was not planning to produce film for motion pictures, but it had resources that allowed it to exploit the opportunity that Edison presented. Edison's invention was an unexpected event, but Kodak was able to seize the opportunity when it emerged, whereas other companies were not.

To make this assessment, a manager must look for historical evidence that the firm has been able to consistently exploit opportunities and neutralize threats when they have emerged. To be consistent with the RBV, the focus should be on resources, not products or services. In the Kodak example, it was not the film that really enabled Kodak to meet the needs of Thomas Edison, because the film was not originally created to fulfill the motion picture niche. Instead, it was the engineering skill (a human and organizational resource owned by Kodak) that allowed it to be innovative and flexible enough to exploit the opportunity that it was not expecting.

Figure 3.10 – Thomas Edison & the kinetoscope (Kodak.com)

❷ *Are the firm's resources rare?*

VRIO analysis is considered to be part of internal analysis, but here we see that it depends also on knowledge of the industry and competitors too. In the second step of the VRIO analysis, a manager must compare the foundational resources controlled by his or her firm to those controlled by other firms in the industry. Specifically, the determination must be made about whether the firm's resources are rare in the industry. The logic of this step is obvious: if a firm has resources that are common (i.e. not rare resources) then it cannot ever hope to establish a sustained competitive advantage. In fact, its best aspirations could only be to achieve parity in its industry. In other words, if the firm builds its strategy on resources that are similar to competitors' resources, then there is no reason to believe that it will accomplish above-average results. In the previous section of this chapter, we discussed the value chain of Dell Computer Corp. At time it was designed, Dell's value chain was rare in the PC industry. Remember that the products themselves are not really unique – the reason Dell was so successful was not due to its products, but its key resources. Its method for acquiring and managing inventory, managing cash flow, then selling directly to the end user are the explanations for Dell's success. It created a value chain that was both valuable and rare.

Consequently Dell achieved a competitive advantage in the industry, but only for awhile. When Dell's business model become successful, Compaq, Gateway, and others imitated what Dell had done.

Table 3.3 shows a summary of the VRIO logic after the first two steps. If a firm's resources are neither valuable nor rare then we would expect it to be uncompetitive in its industry – it would be at a competitive disadvantage relative to its competitors. If it had resources that were valuable but common, it could expect competitive parity or equality in its industry. And if it owned resources that were valuable and rare (like Dell's value chain) it would expect to achieve a temporary competitive advantage.

Table 3.3 – Implications of the Resource Based View of the Firm

If the firm's resources are:	Then the firm can expect:
Neither valuable nor rare	Competitive disadvantage
Valuable but not rare	Competitive parity
Valuable and rare	Temporary competitive advantage

❸ *Are the firm's resources costly or difficult to imitate?*

If a firm has collected resources that are rare (step 2) then the next criteria to consider is whether those resources are difficult to imitate. The more difficult they are to imitate, the longer the firm will be able to maintain its competitive advantage. An important part of managing resources is to prevent competitors from copying, substituting, or replicating the functions of the valuable and rare resources that the firm owns. There are several ways that resources become difficult for competitors to imitate. First, intellectual property laws allow firms to file copyrights, patents, and trademarks on their unique work. Most slogans and logos (e.g. Nike "swoosh") are protected by copyrights and trademarks. The "swoosh" is not the product that Nike sells; it is a resource that the company has designed to represent itself in the market. Anyone who tries to copy the "swoosh" will be violating the copyright and trademark of Nike. So this resource fits the definition of a resource that is difficult for Nike's competitors to imitate.

Second, when resources are "socially complex," according to Barney (1995), they are also difficult for competitors to imitate. Socially complex resources are those that are more effective because they are part of the culture of an organization. The resource itself could possibly be copied, but the performance or effectiveness of the resource cannot be easily imitated. The manufacturing system at Toyota (known as Toyota Production System or TPS) is widely regarded as the reason the company has become the largest car manufacturer in the world. The curious fact about TPS is that many competitors have tried to imitate it, but have been unable to duplicate Toyota's results. Taylor and Kahn offer this description (1997).

> "But why is it, exactly, that nobody has been able to imitate TPS, much less duplicate its results? GM, Ford, and Chrysler have all borrowed bits and pieces, and Honda's system resembles Toyota's in many areas. But nobody has been able to match the master. 'Even though TPS has been studied to death, it is not properly understood,' says John Shook, an American who went to work for Toyota in Japan back in 1983 and now directs the Japan Technology Management Program at the University of Michigan. 'Remember how Vince Lombardi always said he would share his playbook with anyone, but nobody could execute like the old Green Bay Packers? It is the same thing with Toyota. Everybody has techniques and practices, but nobody has a system like Toyota's.'"

Competitors are even allowed to take tours of TPS facilities in the US and Japan. Yet others are not able to imitate the results that Toyota has shown. The reason is that while the competitors are able imitate most of the hardware and assembly line design, they can't duplicate the corporate culture, the training methods, the teamwork, and the camaraderie of Toyota. In other words, the hardware is integrated into the culture, which makes it "socially complex" – nobody can imitate the whole system because they can't really see and understand how all the pieces of the system fit together. In this way, Toyota has made TPS very difficult to imitate.

Third, some resources are difficult to imitate because historical events, or the passage of time, create huge cost disadvantages for companies that try to imitate them. Barney's example (1995) is based on Caterpillar's worldwide distribution system. During WWII the US government requested bids for private contractors to develop a distribution network for delivering heavy machinery around the world. As part of the war effort, the military needed to move equipment quickly, and then put that equipment to use building infrastructure (bridges, roads, airstrips, etc). Caterpillar won the contract, collaborated with the government, and today still reaps the benefits. It has a distribution network that leads the industry. Any competitor of Caterpillar faces a huge cost disadvantage in trying to develop similar resources. It would not be likely to get a government to subsidize the creation of the network, so Caterpillar's resource is very difficult for competitors to imitate. Other companies have captured "first mover advantages" by being early developers of new products, systems or markets. During the early days, those companies can build an advantage based on technical expertise, high market share, cost advantages, long term contracts with vendors or customers, and brand recognition. Future imitators find it very slow and costly to catch up. Steinway & Sons is widely considered the premier piano manufacturer in the world. Many concert pianists will perform live concerts only if a Steinway is provided. The company began building hand-made pianos in the 1860s. Today, it would be virtually impossible for a competitor to begin making pianos using a technique similar to what Steinway has been developing for 150 years. As a reminder, notice the logic of the RBV: this example is focused on the method of making pianos, not the pianos themselves.

❹ *Is the firm organized so that it can fully exploit its resources?*

The last criterion helps determine whether the firm is able to capture the potential advantages that the resources could provide. It is possible that a firm has developed resources that are valuable, rare, and hard to imitate, but then it squanders the potential of its resources. To meet this criteria, there must be evidence that the firm's systems, communication, incentive structure, and corporate culture are designed so that it can make use of the resources that are valuable, rare, and difficult to imitate. For example, the basketball team with the better players does not always win a game. If the players have weak teamwork, poor communication, or bad coaching, the team might lose to a team with inferior players. The same problem can plague an organization: excellent resources don't guarantee excellent performance. The organization must capitalize on the resources that are valuable, rare, and difficult to imitate. There is a famous example of a company that had resources that were valuable, rare, and difficult for competitors to imitate. However, the company was not organized to exploit the resources. In 1973, a division of Xerox invented the world's first personal computer. It had a graphical monitor display, a mouse, Ethernet connectivity, and a laser printer. The device gave Xerox a four to six year lead over IBM in the race to build the first computer affordable to individuals and small businesses. Instead of pursuing the new invention, senior managers decided to discontinue the product. The senior managers considered Xerox to be a photocopier company - the company was not organized it a way that would allow it to pursue an entirely new industry. The heartbreaking story is fully explained in Fumbling the Future (Smith & Alexander, 1999).

Table 3.4 shows the implications for competitive advantage using all four of the criteria for the VRIO Analysis. Using VRIO logic, the goal should be for a firm to modify its resources so that they become more valuable, rarer, harder for competitors to imitate, and more fully exploited by the firm. Then and only then will the firm be able to attain a sustained competitive advantage in its industry.

Table 3.4 – Implications of the Resource Based View of the Firm

If the firm's resources are:	Then the firm can expect:
Valuable, rare, but *easy* to imitate	Temporary competitive advantage
Valuable, rare, and hard to imitate	Sustained competitive advantage (if the firm is organized properly)

Now that the components of the Resource Base View have been explained, this section of Chapter 3 will conclude with an explanation of how to conduct a VRIO Analysis. **The first step** is to identify the company's resources that will be analyzed. Any company has hundreds of resources, but only a small group of resources typically forms the foundation of the company's strategy. The temptation is to choose resources that already are strengths of the company. Instead, a manager should identify the resources that form the basis of the company's strategy. Some foundational resources should be chosen because they represent Key Success Factors in the industry (see chapter 2 for a review of KSFs). For example, for any "bricks & mortar" retailer, location is a foundational resource for the company's strategy. A retailer should be easy to find and located near a large group of customers. Note that a retailer's location might be unfavorable, but location should still be included in the VRIO Analysis because it is foundational to any retailer's strategy. Other resources should be included in the analysis because they contribute unique features to the company's strategy. For example, if a company has a call center that makes outbound sales calls, the employee training program might be a resource to include in the VRIO Analysis. Or if a company claims to have the lowest prices in the market, then its cost-control methods might be a resource to analyze. Any company's resources can be categorized into four groups: physical resources, financial resources, human resources, and organizational resources. A manager should identify one or two resources in each category and make them the focus of the VRIO Analysis. Consequently, the list of resources to analyze should be a minimum of four and a maximum of eight.

The second step is to apply the VRIO logic to each of the company's foundational resources. Returning to the example from step 1 above, imagine a manager conducting a VRIO Analysis of his call center company. As mentioned above, the company's sales training would be a resource that was foundational to the company's strategy. The manager should determine whether the training program is valuable, then whether the training program is rare among the competing call center companies, then whether the characteristics of the training program would be difficult for competitors to imitate, and finally, whether the company was organized so that it fully exploited its training program. If the manager applied the VRIO logic to the sales training program and answered 'yes' to each question, then he could conclude that the sale training program was a source of sustained competitive advantage for the company. If the analysis indicated that a resource did not meet all four criteria, then the competitive implication is that the resource would not contribute to creating a sustained competitive advantage for the company. See Table 3.5 for an illustration that summarizes a fictitious VRIO Analysis.

After conducting a VRIO Analysis on each of the company's foundational resources, **the third step** is to consider the strategic changes that are warranted by the analysis. Specifically, the VRIO should give a manager some guidance on what aspects of each resource could be improved.

Table 3.5 – Summary of a Fictional VRIO Analysis

Resource	Valuable?	Rare?	Costly to Imitate?	Exploited?	Competitive Implications
Sales Training Program	Y	Y	N	Y	Temporary Competitive Advantage
Resource #2	Y	Y	N	N	Competitive Parity
Resource #3	N	N	N	N	Competitive Disadvantage

Returning to the example, look at the first row in Table 3.5. The VRIO Analysis for "sales training program" was found to be valuable and rare, but not difficult to imitate. In other words, the company has designed training for its sales people that enables the company to exploit opportunities and neutralize threats (i.e. the definition of 'valuable'). Additionally, the training program is unique in the industry – few other companies provide training that is similar. As an aside – notice that in order to make such a conclusion, a manager would need to know a lot of information about the company's competitors in the industry. The third criterion for VRIO asks whether the resource is difficult to imitate. In this example, the answer is No. The manager believes that other companies could easily copy or duplicate the sales training program. Anywhere a 'no' answer occurs during a VRIO Analysis, managers can ask how the 'no' can be changed into a 'yes'. In this example, the manager should ask how the sales training program could be made more difficult to imitate. If he really believes the program is valuable and rare, the company should see the incentive for keeping it out of the hands of competitors. Some obvious suggestions might be to copyright the training manual, to reduce employee turnover so that 'leaks' are reduced, to regularly upgrade the training so that old versions become obsolete quickly, or to integrate the training into the corporate culture so that it becomes too complex to imitate. This same approach applies to any situation when a company has a resource that does not meet all four criteria of a VRIO Analysis. According to the Resource Based View, an organization can only create a sustainable competitive advantage when it has resources that are valuable, rare, difficult for competitors to imitate, and is organized so that it can exploit its resources.

Conclusion and Preview of Chapter 4

Chapter 3 presented the details of Internal Analysis, which corresponds to section 2.b) of the Strategy Process Cycle (see Figure 1.3). The one-word motto for this section is "Learn," which indicates that managers should have learned all the key features of the industry and the company's competencies in this section. To pass through the second gate, managers must have developed a clear understanding of whether the organization has a competitive advantage and if so, the source or foundation of the advantage. The three components of internal analysis presented in this chapter were 1) financial ratio analysis, 2) value chain analysis, and 3) VRIO analysis. In the next chapter, the book will cover strategy formulation and the three interdependent levels of strategy.

For Further Consideration

The term "energy independence" was an important topic in the 2008 and 2012 U.S. presidential elections. The U.S. has been a major oil importer for many years, and politicians recognize the risk of being dependent on imported oil & gas for the country's energy needs. In response, energy companies have been developing new sources of domestic oil and natural gas. In fact, in world markets, the U.S. has developed a competitive advantage in natural gas production. According to Gold & Kruk (2012) "The advantages that the U.S. enjoys from its shale boom are the envy of the rest of the world – the U.S. is moving toward some kind of energy self-reliance, and domestic prices have fallen to a point where industrial end-users have reliable, cheap energy."

Figure 3.11

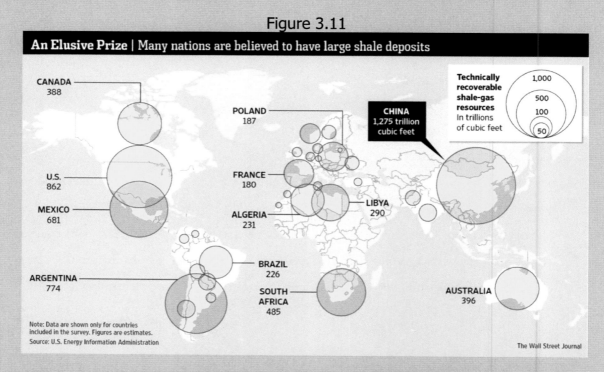

Figure 3.11 shows the estimated shale gas deposits in several countries. The U.S. has substantial deposits of gas, but other companies have similar (or even more) quantities of natural gas. Yet the U.S. is expected to have a competitive advantage in gas production until about 2022. Gas is a commodity product – the quality is similar in all markets in the world. What explains the competitive advantage that the U.S. has created?

For a response, skip forward two pages to "Answers for Review and Discussion"

Questions for Review & Discussion

1. In the table below, match the restaurant activity in the left column to the appropriate value chain activity in the right column.

Restaurant Activity	Corresponding Value Chain Label
A. Purchasing ingredients	Sales & marketing
B. Delivering meals to the table, car, or home	Inbound logistics
C. Preparing the meal	Operations
D. Radio advertising	Outbound logistics

2. Match the financial ratios in the left column to the appropriate formula to calculate the ratio in the right column.

Financial Ratio	Formula
A. Net Profit Margin	Current Assets / Current Liabilities
B. Return on Investment	Net Profit / Total Revenue
C. Asset Turnover	Total Revenue / Total Assets
D. Current Ratio	Net Profit / Total Assets
E. Quick Ratio	(Current Assets – Inventory) / Current Liabilities

Answers for Review & Discussion

1.

A. Purchasing ingredients = inbound logistics

Inbound Logistics includes all the activities that help acquire the supplies and inputs that the organization needs to conduct its operations. In addition to acquiring the inputs, inbound logistics includes storing and managing the inventory of the inputs. In organizations that buy and handle inputs that are bulky, expensive, or perishable, this activity can be a critical and expensive activity. For any business that is based on products, Inbound Logistics is clearly a key activity. For a restaurant, this activity includes identifying food wholesalers and distributors for all its ingredients.

B. Delivering meals to the table, car, or home = outbound logistics

Outbound Logistics occurs as the output from operations is delivered or transferred to the next customer in the chain of activities. As with the first two activities, the composition of this activity varies widely from industry to industry and even from company to company within the same industry. In some industries outbound logistics requires an output to be delivered only a short distance over a short period of time. The restaurant industry is a good example of this situation. Food is delivered to a customer across a counter, or by a waiter who carries the food to a table. Many restaurants have home delivery service, so outbound logistics is a little more complicated

C. Preparing the meal = operations

Operations is probably the most encompassing of the Primary Activities. Everything that helps transform inputs into outputs falls into the Operations activity. For most organizations, operations is the heart of what creates the most value for the end user. Using the restaurant example from the previous paragraph, operations begins with menu planning and design, recipe selection, and concludes with food preparation.

D. radio advertising = sales & marketing

Sales & Marketing includes the activities the organization uses for receiving and sending information about all its markets.

2.

    A. Net Profit Margin = net profit / total revenue
    B. Return on Investment = net profit / total assets
    C. Asset Turnover = total revenue / total assets
    D. Current Ratio = current assets / current liabilities
    E. Quick Ratio = (current Assets – inventory) / current liabilities

For Further Consideration (Continued)

The US natural gas industry is a great example of the Resource-Based View. Natural gas is a commodity product, so it can't be why the US has created an advantage. Natural gas in the US is identical to natural gas found in other countries. The difference is the resources that the US industry has in <u>extracting</u> the gas and <u>transporting</u> the gas. Geological data in the US far surpasses that in Russia and South America. Consequently, even in countries with massive reserves of natural gas, the geological expertise might be insufficient for the gas to be extracted. Second, the US has an excellent infrastructure for moving natural gas from the source to the refineries. Other countries, even when they can extract the gas, have trouble moving it safely into markets where it can be refined and consumed.

References

Barney, J. (1995). Looking inside for competitive advantage. *Academy of Management Executive*, Vol. 9 (4): 49 – 61.

Bennett, D. (2019). They're coming for your eyeballs. *Bloomberg BusinessWeek*. May 13: 38-45.

Crain, D. & Abraham, S. (2008). Using value-chain analysis to discover customers' strategic needs. *Strategy & Leadership*, 36: 29-39.

Gold, R. & Kruk, M. (2012). Global gas push stalls. *Wall Street Journal*, December 3, p. A1.

Hertzer, M. (2019). Donald Trump's threat to close Mexico border sends avocado prices soaring. Fortune, April 3. http://fortune.com/2019/04/03/trump-mexico-border-avocado-price/ Accessed 6/10/19.

Kaplan, R. & Norton, D. (1996). *The Balanced Scorecard: Translating Strategy into Action*.. Harvard Business Press, Boston.

Kinni, T., Ilona, S., Worthen, B. (2008). Capturing the People Advantage: Thought leaders on Human Capital. Booz, Allen, Hamilton.

Love, J. (1987). Big Macs, fries, and real estate." *Financial Executive*. April, #4: 20-26.

Porter, M.E. (1980). *Competitive Strategy: Techniques for Analyzing Industries and Competitors*. New York: The Free Press.

Preiss, K., Goldman, S., Nagel, R. (1996). *Cooperate to Compete: Building Agile Business Relationships.* John Wiley: New York.

Shaich, R. (2008). Letter to Stockholders in Panera Bread Company Annual Report. Accessed 4/1/09 at www.panera.com.

Taylor, A. & Kahn, J. (1997). How Toyota defies gravity. *Fortune*. December 8. www.money.cnn.com/magazines/fortune/fortune_archive/1997/12/08/234926/index.htm

UPS Website. http://www.ups-scs.com/logistics/distribution_network.html. Accessed 5/20/09.

Yanushevsky, C. (2019). *Industry Surveys: Retail*. CFRA: New York. www.capitaliq.com. Accessed 6/10/19.

Chapter 4:
Corporate-level & Business-level Strategy

At this point in the book, we finally turn to the topic of formulating strategy. Until this time, the book has discussed how to set the goals and aspirations of an organization (dream), and how to analyze the organization's current situation (learn), Figure 4.1 is a reproduction of the Strategy Process Cycle that has guided the content so far.

Figure 4.1 - The Strategy Process Cycle

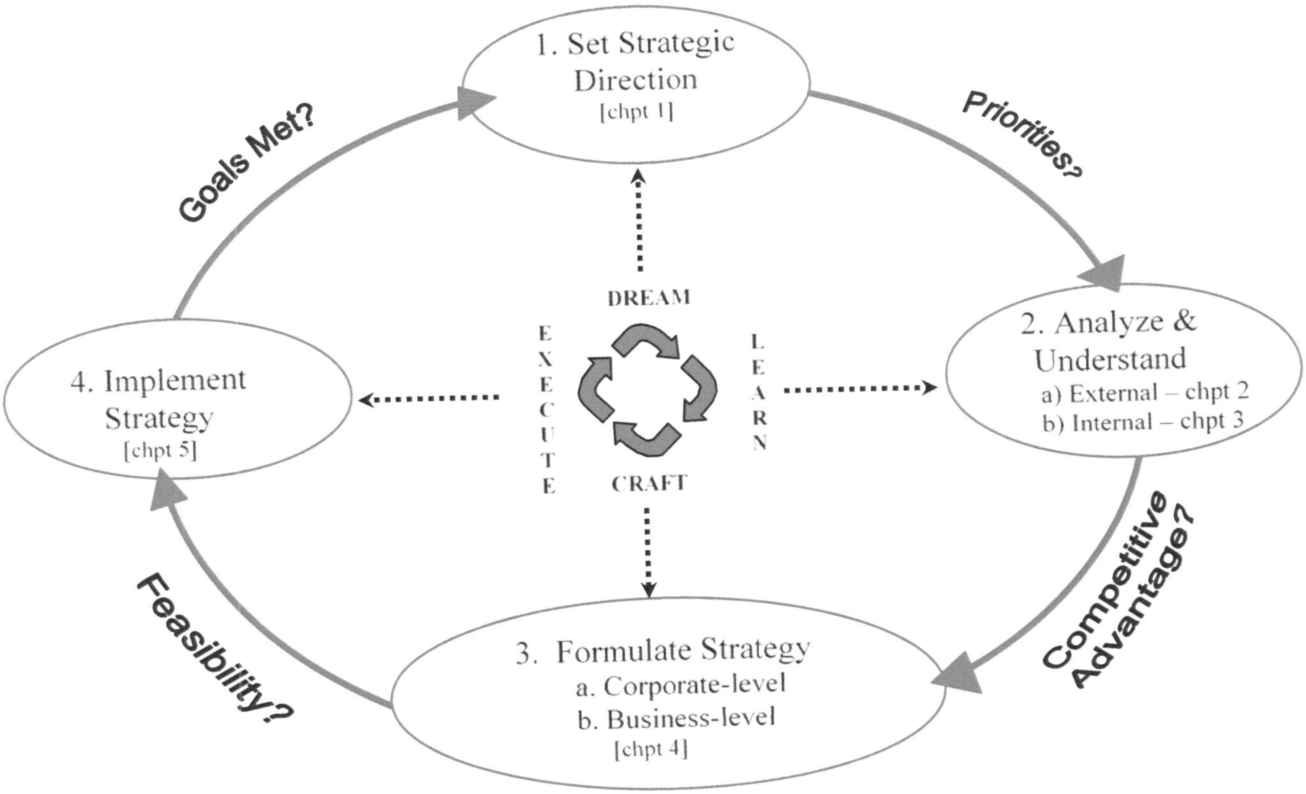

At the conclusion of step 2 in the Strategy Process Cycle, managers should be confident in their knowledge of the organization's competitive advantage. Once the company's competitive advantage has been identified, leaders are prepared for step 3, which is to design the company's strategy.

Unlike the courses in the functional areas of business (e.g. marketing or finance), strategic management takes a perspective of the whole organization. Consequently, the concept of strategy must also address the whole organization. For this reason we recognize that strategy must be formulated at three interdependent levels. This chapter is divided into two sections, each of which will address one level of strategy.

<u>Learning Objectives for Chapter 4</u>:

1. Distinguish between corporate, business, and functional levels of strategy
2. Evaluate a company's diversification strategy using a portfolio matrix model
3. Identify a company's strategy using a generic strategy matrix.

Opening Vignette for Chapter 4

An important and difficult component of strategy is having divisions in a company work cooperatively, interdependently, and synergistically. Later in the chapter, you will learn about the concept of *related diversification*, a corporate-level strategy that requires divisions to become less autonomous and find ways to create value for each other. For years, Time Warner Inc. tried to encourage cooperation among its business units. It owned successful media and entertainment brands like CNN, HBO, and Cartoon Network. They created famous products like "Sopranos" and "Game of Thrones." Over the years, there were plans to collaborate on projects. One was called Project Scooby – named after the Warner Bros. cartoon character. An anonymous executive said "I couldn't remember many times over the years where we'd have all three companies deciding strategy together" (Flint & Benjamin, 2019). Project Scooby and many others never resulted in any meaningful collaboration across the business units. Finally, in June of 2018, the company got a jolt that is leading to some success for the companies working together. AT&T bought the company for $84.5 billion so it could begin to compete with Disney, Netflix, and Amazon in the creation *and* delivery of entertainment content. The company was re-branded as WarnerMedia, there was some executive turnover, and CEO of AT&T (John Stankey) required firm plans on how the companies would collaborate. Figure 4.2 shows the "before and after" portfolio of AT&T.

Figure 4.2:
AT&T Acquisition of Time Warner, Inc. in 2018

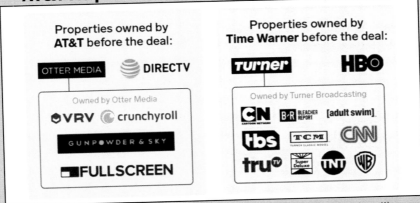

Source: https://www.businessinsider.com/att-time-warner-acquisition-what-it-will-own-2018-6

The first plan for collaboration was a streaming subscription service to compete with Netflix. The center of the service would be HBO content, but content from other brands will be available too, such as Cartoon Network and Warner Bros., which owns film series like Harry Potter, Batman, and The Hobbit.

Before the acquisition, AT&T was primarily a distributor of entertainment through cable TV, cell phone service, and DirecTV. After the acquisition, it also owns the entertainment content so it is well-positioned to compete with Netflix and Disney.

Levels of Strategy

Figure 4.3 shows the former organizational structure of PepsiCo. PepsiCo bought Pizza Hut in 1977, Taco Bell in 1978, and KFC in 1986. The three restaurants were one part of the overall strategy of PepsiCo to be a global food service company. But in 1997 PepsiCo decided to spin-off its entire restaurant division as a separate company called Tricon. In 2002 Tricon changed its name to Yum! Brands.

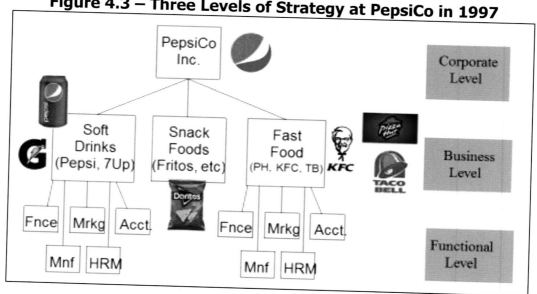

Figure 4.3 – Three Levels of Strategy at PepsiCo in 1997

CORPORATE-LEVEL STRATEGY

Scope of Corporate-level strategy

The corporate level of strategy sets the overall direction for the whole company. There are specific tasks to accomplish and questions to answer that are unique to the corporate level of strategy. Stated as questions, the scope of corporate level strategy is:

- In how many industries should we compete?
- How should resources be allocated across our portfolio of businesses?
- What synergy exists across our portfolio of businesses?
- What overseas markets are promising?

The corporate-level strategic decisions at PepsiCo are reflected in Figure 4.3. In the early 1970s PepsiCo was competing in just two industries – soft drinks and snack foods (purchased Frito-Lay in 1965). In 1977 senior executives changed their answer to the first question of corporate-level strategy ("in how many industries should we compete?"). With the purchase of Pizza Hut, PepsiCo began competing in <u>three</u> separate industries. What was the logic for this change? Two reasons are obvious. First, investment in the restaurant business constituted forward vertical integration (see **Figure 2.4** for a review). The fast food chains would serve only PepsiCo beverages, so the restaurants represented a captive audience of consumers. Everyone who ate a meal at Pizza Hut, KFC, or Taco Bell would also be buying beverages made by Pepsi. Second, corporate-level managers at PepsiCo probably recognized the growth potential of the fast food industry in the mid-1970s. That was a time when two-income families become more popular, so families were eating meals in restaurants more than ever before. The second question ("How should resources be allocated?") is harder to examine at PepsiCo, but we can imagine why the question is important. Every organization is constrained by limited resources. Imagine if the brand managers for Diet Pepsi and Doritos make competing requests for funding a really expensive TV ad during the Super Bowl. How do corporate-level managers make the decision about allocating advertising dollars across the three business units? This scenario is a fictional example, but it illustrates the dilemma that corporate managers face when they work on corporate level strategy. The third issue, synergy, is easy to see at PepsiCo. Synergy is often defined as occurring when "the whole is greater than the sum of the parts" and can be achieved when corporate managers find ways for business units to cooperate and share resources. Maximizing the *combined* performance of the corporation is the main goal of corporate-level strategy. Selling Pepsi beverages inside PepsiCo restaurants is an example of creating synergy that was discussed earlier. Another obvious synergy could be in cross-advertising (e.g. Taco Bell promoting and selling Frito-Lay brand corn chips and salsa). Fourth, most overseas expansions are considered as part of the corporate-level strategy. International strategy is an obvious part of PepsiCo's success as it was one of the leaders in growing franchisee revenue in overseas markets beginning in the 1970s.

As a continuation of the PepsiCo example, fast-forward to 1997. That year PepsiCo sold its entire fast food business unit, spinning it off under the new name Tricon. That decision is an interesting illustration of corporate-level strategy. At the time, Pizza Hut was the market share leader in the pizza segment of the fast food industry, Taco Bell was the market share leader in the Mexican food segment, and KFC was the market share leader in the chicken segment. Furthermore, the fast food business unit contributed about half of PepsiCo's total corporate revenue and more than half of total corporate profits. An obvious discussion question is: **Why did PepsiCo sell its fast food division?** We will cover the concept of "related diversification" first, and then return to this question later in the chapter.

Diversification

In the context of corporate-level strategy, the concept of diversification has the same meaning as in finance: it is the process of investing in businesses or assets in other industries. For most of its history, PepsiCo was not diversified – it was only a manufacturer of carbonated beverages. In 1965 it diversified into snack foods with the purchase of Frito-Lay, Inc., and then diversified again in 1977 when it purchased Pizza Hut. The primary logic for pursuing diversification is to spread risk across different industries. In finance, investors are advised to diversify their portfolios so they have exposure to many different industries and investment vehicles (e.g. some bonds, some utility stocks, some blue chip stocks, some tech stocks, some precious metal stocks, some cash, etc.). In corporate-level strategy, the same logic applies, but we also characterize the *amount* or *degree* of diversification that a company is pursuing. <u>Concentric</u> diversification is when a company invests in another industry that is related to its core business and <u>conglomerate</u> diversification is when the investment is not related to the core business. However, the characterization is not a dichotomous, "either/or" choice. A simple way to characterize diversification is on a continuum anchored on each end by the two extreme forms of diversification. See Figure 4.4

Figure 4.4 – Continuum of Diversification Strategy

Conglomerate
Diversification
(unrelated)

Concentric
Diversification
(related)

On the far left of the scale is conglomerate diversification, when a firm invests in another firm and the two have almost nothing in common – there is no "relatedness" between the two. Famous examples of companies pursuing this corporate level strategy are General Electric and Berkshire Hathaway. GE manufactures diesel locomotives, light bulbs, consumer appliances, saltwater desalination plants, and jet aircraft engines. Berkshire Hathaway is a holding company that invests in companies with good management and typically leaves the managers in place after the acquisition. It owns part or all of companies such as Acme Brick Company, Fruit of the Loom, NetJets, and Geico Auto Insurance.

Concentric Diversification

A famous example on the other end of the scale (related diversification) is BIC Corporation. Most people know BIC for its familiar products: disposable shavers & razors, lighters, and pens. At first glance it might seem that BIC is also pursuing unrelated diversification, because those three products are obviously in distinct industries. From the consumer's perspective, shaving, writing, and lighting cigarettes or candles are activities that have nothing in common. So it might be tempting to characterize BIC's strategy as unrelated or conglomerate diversification. However, the "relatedness" of the products is not the best criteria to use when examining a company's corporate-level strategy. Instead of looking at "product relatedness" for evidence of the synergy between business units, Ilinitch and Zeithaml (1995) proposed looking at "managerial relatedness," defined as "'similarities in organizational structure, management processes, dominant functions, succession paths, and management beliefs and values" (p. 402).

In the case of BIC Corporation, what managerial relatedness exists across the business units of pens, razors, and lighters? What activities can be shared or leveraged across the three business units?

First, the customers and distribution channels are the same for all three of BIC's business units. Pens, razors, and lighters are sold to grocery stores, drug stores, and convenience stores. The products are disposable and 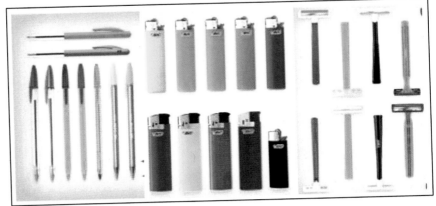 are often purchased on impulse when consumers see them on the shelves and remember that they need to re-stock. **Second**, there are some similarities in the process of manufacturing all three products. They are simple products, made mostly of plastic, produced in mass quantity in highly automated facilities. BIC probably uses many of the same companies as vendors for its three divisions. Plastic can be purchased in large quantities, then distributed to the manufacturing

Chapter 4: Corporate & Business Level Strategy

facilities. Because of these similarities, there are likely to be lessons, skills, and resources that can be shared across the business units. **Third**, the human resource management function is likely to be similar in all three businesses because the jobs are likely to be similar – production managers and assembly line workers. Recruiting, training, and development tasks can be developed at the corporate level and deployed in all three business units. These three examples are obvious illustrations of how BIC Corporation's corporate-level strategy is related diversification. The three business units produce products that are not similar from the consumer's perspective, but there are many skills, competencies, and resources that BIC can leverage to capture synergy across its portfolio.

In general, the strengths of related diversification are based on economies of scope, which occurs when an organization is able to lower its average unit costs because it spreads its costs across a range of revenue-generating activities. The concept is similar to economies of scale, but depends on adding a range of activities per unit cost instead of unit costs being lowered by increased volume. For example, the marginal costs of running a second, related business would not double the total costs of both businesses. This is true because 1) some overhead costs can be eliminated by operating two or more businesses under the same corporate entity, 2) some activities along the value chain can create value for both businesses, while incurring only one cost.

More specific approaches to pursuing related diversification and capturing economies of scope are shown in Table 4.1. All the approaches have a similarity: they allow a company to become more cost competitive or strategically competitive by combining or sharing some resources across two or more business units. After this discussion of the definition and benefits of related diversification, let's return to the question about PepsiCo's corporate-level strategy in 1997 (see Figure 4.3). The question posed earlier in the chapter was about the logic behind Pepsi's divestiture of its fast food division – why would the company sell the biggest and most profitable of its three divisions? To answer the question, we should consider the "relatedness" of the three business units in PepsiCo's portfolio. Table 4.2 shows a quick comparison of the value chains of the three units.

Table 4.1 – Approaches to Related Diversification

Approach	Example company	Details
Share salesmen or distribution channels	PepsiCo	Both business units (snack foods & soft drinks) sell to grocery stores and other retailers. Distribution and shipping can be shared across the units.
Share similar technologies	Honda Corp.	Gasoline engines are the core product in all business units: cars, lawn mowers, generators, scooters, etc.
Transfer expertise from one unit to another	UPS	Expertise in the shipping industry led to creating services for managing customers' entire logistics systems.
Transfer brand name from one unit to another	Google	Reputation as the best internet search engine helps create trust for people to use Chrome, Google's web browser.
Acquire a business for the purpose of improving the outcomes of existing business	Cisco / WebEx	Cisco acquired WebEx in 2007 ($3.2b) because WebEx created an on-line collaboration tool that integrated well with Cisco's internet hubs and switches.
Share common suppliers / raw materials	BIC Corp.	All three business units manufacture products made primarily from plastic. Raw materials purchasing can be centralized & coordinated across the three units.

Based on the information in Table 4.2 it becomes easier to determine why PepsiCo sold its fast food unit. When comparing the value chains of the three units, fast food does not have the same level of strategic fit as do the snack food and soft drink units. In short, running three chains of franchised fast food restaurants is a very different business than manufacturing chips and soft drinks. With the fast food unit in the portfolio, there are fewer opportunities for synergy and economies of scope to develop across all the business units. We can use Figure 4.3 to plot the change in diversification strategy for PepsiCo. When the fast food unit was sold, PepsiCo returned to its corporate-level strategy from 1977, before it purchased Pizza Hut (its first investment in the fast food industry).

Table 4.2 – Comparison of PepsiCo's Business Units, 1997

Value Chain Activity	Business Unit		
	Snack Foods	Soft Drinks	Fast Food
Operations	Manufacturer	Manufacturer	Restaurant chain
Sales / customer focus	Grocery & convenience	Grocery & convenience	Individual consumer
HRM	FT employees - careers	FT employees – careers	PT workers; franchise
Inbound logistics	Buy bulk raw materials	Buy bulk raw materials	Buy frozen food
Administration	Manage big factories	Manage big factories	Manage retail venues

Figure 4.5 plots the change in PepsiCo's corporate-level strategy. On the continuum, P87 shows PepsiCo in 1987 after it had completed the purchase of all three fast food brands. The investment in the fast food industry positioned PepsiCo about midway between a concentric and a conglomerate strategy. All its businesses were in the food industry and the restaurants were customers of the soft drink industry, so there was some opportunity for synergy and economies of scope. But as illustrated in Table 4.2 there was much dissimilarity in the three business units. P97 represents the corporate-level strategy of PepsiCo after the fast food unit was divested and spun off as Tricon in 1997. The new strategy is a strong shift toward the concentric diversification end of the continuum. Becoming less diversified is described by Hoskinsson and Hitt (1994) as "downscoping, which refocuses the firm on its primary core businesses, allowing it to regain strategic control" (p. 195).

Figure 4.5 – Plot of the change in PepsiCo's Corporate-Level Strategy

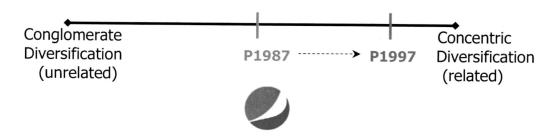

Conglomerate Diversification (unrelated)   P1987 ----------> P1997   Concentric Diversification (related)

Conglomerate Diversification

In spite of the benefits of related (concentric) diversification, many firms pursue a corporate-level strategy of unrelated (conglomerate) diversification. However, unrelated diversification may have reached its peak in popularity during the merger fad during the 1960s and 1970s. "Corporate restructuring in the 1980s has generally been seen as an 'undoing' of the conglomerate merger wave of the 1960s and 1970s. In the consensus view, the last 30 years has been a …..trip from specialization to conglomeration and back to specialization or 'focus' (Klein, 2001: 745). Even today, there are typically a handful of reasons why unrelated diversification is pursued by companies hoping to become more competitive.

Risk reduction is probably the most common reason given for why firms diversify into industries that have little in common with their core business. "By spreading investments across several industries a firm is subject to less risk: cash flow is more stable over time" (Sadler, Ryall & Craig, 2003:104). Modern finance theory has clearly documented the benefits of creating a diversified portfolio for enhancing the expected return of the portfolio. However, most of the benefits of diversification can be accomplished with related diversification without the added complexity of managing employees and strategy in businesses with no meaningful value chain overlaps.

Economies of scope in corporate services can occur when a firm has excess capacity in its headquarters facility. These capabilities could be in legal expertise, brand building, sales training, IT infrastructure development, etc. In this view, the headquarters office acts like a consulting firm, providing special support and advice to its portfolio companies that create value even if there are no operational synergies between the business units.

Providing efficient internal capital markets is based on the idea that business units compete with each other to gather resources allocated by the corporate decision makers. If each business unit is a profit center, then one role of the corporate office is to impose financial discipline by rewarding successful profit centers and giving them resources to continue to grow. Conversely, weaker business units will be less likely to deserve capital and may eventually be divested. If the business units were independent, they would rely on the external capital market to provide funding for growth and investment. By competing instead in the internal capital market, the business units have some advantages. In the external capital markets, there are usually large transaction costs associated with conducting due diligence, hiring attorneys, and vetting the recipient of capital. Second, internal capital markets have much better information about the status and competitiveness of each business unit

Acquiring companies with undervalued equity is used as a justification for unrelated diversification when managers believe they can buy a company at a discount to its true worth. Even if the target company has no resources or competencies that "fit" with the strategy of the acquiring company, it is possible to "buy low and sell high," just as individual investors try to do with buying and selling in the stock market.

Probably the most familiar company to use a conglomerate diversification strategy is General Electric. "GE had moved in and out of businesses since 1892: airplane engines, plastics, cannons, computers, MRI machines, oil-field drill bits, water-desalination units, television shows, movies,

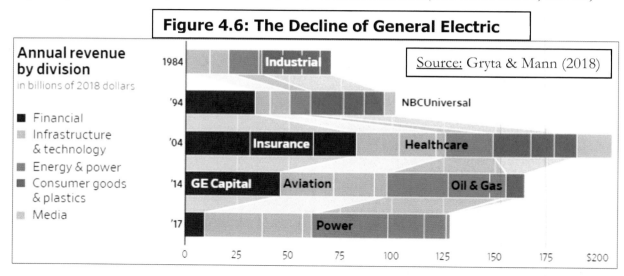

Figure 4.6: The Decline of General Electric

credit cards and insurance. The big machines were always GE's beating heart. But it was a willingness to expand into growing businesses and shed weaker ones that helped make it the rare conglomerate to survive the mass extinction of its rivals" (Gryra & Mann, 2018). As global competition increased in all its industries, GE managers found that unrelated diversification became more complex than ever before. Buying and selling companies under the GE umbrella became a weak substitute for having a strategy that integrated all the business units together. See Figure 4.6 for a summary of the slow decline in revenue of GE in the last 15 years. In 2004, its insurance business (Genworth Financial) and consumer finance division (GE Capital) were large and profitable. By 2017, only two large businesses remained: jet aircraft engines and electric power generators.

Single Business Strategy

Up to this point in Chapter 4, the discussion of corporate-level strategy has concentrated on diversification. As firms grow and mature, they often diversify into other industries. But not always. The benefits of diversification have been discussed earlier in the chapter, but pursing a single business strategy also has merit. Some large, successful, and famous companies have decided to invest almost all their assets in a single industry. Notable examples are Southwest Airlines and McDonald's. There are several reasons why some companies choose to focus on a single industry. A single-minded focus on one clear mission sends a clear message to employees and customers. In single business firms, there is less likely to be ambiguity about the purpose, goals, or scope of the organization. McDonald's is famous for the "golden arches" that are recognized worldwide. Does anyone doubt what those arches stand for? Probably not. Compare the scope of McDonald's to that of another famous company, Nike. Nike's business is harder to classify. Is it a shoe company, a golf club manufacturer, or a sporting goods retailer? The answer, of course, is that Nike competes in all of those industries and others too. While Nike enjoys the benefit of reduced risk via diversification, McDonald's never leaves any doubt about which industry it has created. Developing resources and competencies in single business firm is probably easier than in a diversified firm. Because the mission and product line is unambiguous, it is easier to know what skill are required and what gaps exist in current skill sets.

Competition for resource allocation between business units is not a diversion in single-business companies. The internal capital markets (discussed above) are thought to be an efficient market for most diversified companies, but there are transaction costs too. Single businesses do not face the dilemma of machining either/or choices to allocate resources to one business unit instead of the other.

Performance Implications of Corporate-Level Strategy

Among all the strategic management research topics conducted globally, diversification is one of the most popular. Specifically, authors have wondered which of the three corporate-level strategies is associated with the best company performance. As described in this chapter, there are compelling reasons to believe that single business, related diversification, and unrelated diversification offer the best long-term financial results. While there is not a perfect accord, the consensus view is illustrated in Figure 4.7 (Cyriac, Koller, & Thomsen, 2012).

Figure 4.7 – Relationship between Diversification and Firm Performance

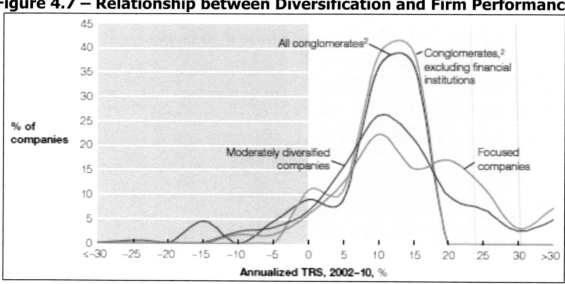

Firms pursuing related diversification generate average performance that is greater than firms pursuing either single-business strategy or unrelated diversification. Single-business firms have "all their eggs in one basket" and over the long run, their higher risk asset allocation does not perform as well as a diversified portfolio. Unrelated diversification tends to trail behind related diversification because managing a complex portfolio of unrelated businesses has proven to be too complicated for most corporate-level managers. The cost of being really diverse seems to be greater than the benefits. Figure 4.6 shows the total return to shareholders (TRS) for companies following 3 different strategies: focused (single business), moderately diversified (related diversification), and conglomerate. According to the authors "diversification often caps the upside potential for shareholders but doesn't limit the downside risk" Cyriac, Koller, & Thomsen, 2012:3). In addition to limiting the companies' upside potential, unrelated diversification also delivered lower mean TRS during 2002-2010.

Throughout Chapter 4, we have studied PepsiCo's decision to diversify into the fast food industry and then divest the fast food division. The overarching task of corporate-level strategy is to manage a portfolio of businesses so that together they perform greater than they would if they were managed independently. In this last section on corporate-level strategy we will review a common technique that managers use for guiding their decisions on investing and divesting within a portfolio. There are two evaluations that must be made about a corporation's portfolio of business units. About each business unit, the following questions should be asked. First, what is the strength of the business unit relative to its competitors in the industry? Second, how attractive is the industry in which the business unit competes? Figure 4.8 shows one version of a matrix that is commonly used to arrange a corporation's business units on a single grid. In a sense, answering these two questions is a culmination of chapter 2 (external analysis) and chapter 3 (internal analysis) of this textbook.

Figure 4.8 – Corporate Strategy Portfolio Matrix

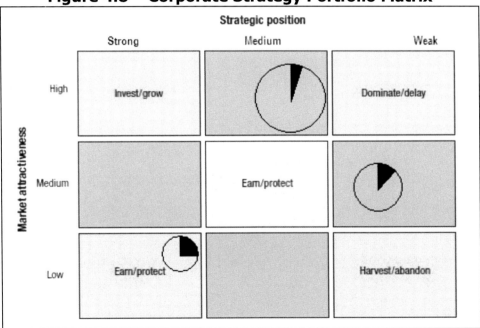

The vertical axis (y-axis) indicates whether the business unit is part of an industry that has high, medium, or low attractiveness. This analysis is exactly the same as what was prescribed when conducting an external analysis in chapter 2. As a reminder, chapter 2 is divided into five interdependent methods for analyzing an industry. Those methods are:

1) Economic conditions of the industry

2) Five Forces Analysis

3) Key Success Factors

4) Strategic Group Analysis

5) Driving Forces Analysis

Of course the industry of each business unit must be assessed independently. So if a corporation has business units competing in four different industries, then corporate-level managers must conduct a unique industry analysis on each.

The horizontal axis (x-axis) indicates whether the business unit has a weak, medium, or strong position in its industry. This analysis is exactly the topic of chapter 3, which was divided into three interdependent methods:

1) Financial ratio analysis

2) Value chain analysis

3) VRIO analysis

Once each business unit has been evaluated, it should be displayed as a circle in the corresponding cell of the nine cell matrix. Two conventions are usually recommended when placing each business unit on the matrix. First, the size of the circle should approximate the size of the industry in which the business competes. The absolute size is not important, but each circle should illustrate the size of the industry relative to the size of the other industries in which the corporation has invested. So if business unit #1 competes in a $1 billion industry and business unit #2 competes in a $500 million industry, circle 1 should be double the size of circle 2. Second, each circle should have a shaded pie wedge that indicates the market share of the business unit being represented. See Figure 4.7 for three examples of fictitious business units and their shaded pie slices.

After each of the corporation's business units have been evaluated and plotted onto the matrix, the next step is to examine the entire portfolio and consider how corporate resources should be allocated to the units. Corporate managers must decide if any business units in the far right column (weak strategic position) are worth pursuing, or should be divested. The cell in the bottom right corner is the best candidate for divesting or abandoning. It occupies a weak position in an unattractive industry. A business unit in the lower left cell is sometimes called a "cash cow" because it probably generates more cash than it needs to operate, so it can be used to fund units in other quadrants that need cash for additional investment. The prescription for the upper right corner is dominate/delay which indicates the dilemma managers face when deciding how to manage a business unit in this situation. The ideal result would be to invest in the business and move it toward the right – into a dominant position in the industry. Realistically, the industry is probably very competitive (since it is attractive) so delaying any investment might make sense if managers think it would not be financially wise to invest into a weak company facing strong competition. Of course the prescriptions in the matrix are only suggestions for guiding managers' decisions. The main takeaway is that there should be a method for examining the whole portfolio of business units that the corporation owns.

BUSINESS-LEVEL STRATEGY

Scope of Business-level strategy

At the business level, managers make different decisions than they make at the corporate level. The tasks and questions are unique to each level. Business-level strategy is concerned with managing the business unit to compete successfully against rivals in the industry. Stated as questions, the scope of business-level strategy is

- What competitive advantage do we have in this industry?
- How do we gain market share?
- What skills & resources still need to be developed?

Since his 1980 book *Competitive Strategy*, Dr. Michael Porter has been considered one of the originators of the concept of business level strategy. At that time, he simplified the concept of strategy to two fundamental issues: leaders must determine the competitive *scope* and the *competitive* advantage of their company. When determining a competitive scope and competitive advantage, the concept of choice is important. Managers must explicitly choose what activities to pursue and what activities to not pursue. Under conditions of scare resources, good strategy requires wise choices and trade-offs. Much earlier in the book (chpt 1) we presented the Five Elements of Strategy – see Figure 4.9 for a review. Making choices about each of these five elements can be informed by the choice about competitive scope and competitive advantage.

Figure 4.9: The Five Elements of Strategy

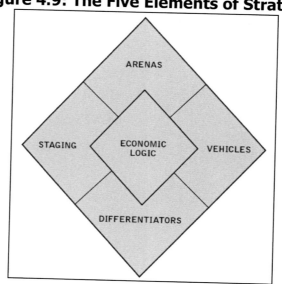

Competitive Scope

Scope refers to the breadth of operations that the company is pursuing, and can be measured along several dimensions. The geographic scope of a strategy refers to the number of markets or regions in which the company operates. A company that sells, manufacturers, or distributes in all the major global markets has chosen a broad geographic scope. Conversely, a company might choose to operate its business within one neighborhood of one city. The geographic scope of most businesses falls somewhere between these two extremes. Second, competitive scope can be defined demographically. In this case, a company makes choices about which customers to purse based on their age, gender, socioeconomic status, or race. Instead of believing that every human is a potential customer, a company should identify the type of people who are most likely to appreciate the value that the product creates. Third, scope can be set according to psychographics, in which potential customers are targeted according to their lifestyles, values, and attitudes. For example, there's a small company in Colorado named Big Agnes. It manufactures and markets only tents, duffel bags, sleeping bags, and sleeping pads. The customers of Big Agnes can't be targeted according to age or race. In other words, there is no demographic scope that is useful for segmenting the market. It makes more sense to segment the market according to people who have hiking and camping as a hobby or lifestyle, irrespective of their race, age, or gender. The product line breadth of a company is another method for defining competitive scope. Some companies choose to offer almost all types of products in the industry whereas others have chosen to focus on a more narrow range of products. As mentioned earlier, Big Agnes has four distinct products. Kelty is a competitor in the same industry. It sells the same four products as Big Agnes but also sells backpacks, baby strollers, and outdoor furniture. So Kelty has seven major product lines and Big Agnes has four major product lines. See Figure 4.10 for a comparison of the two product lines.

Figure 4.10 – Big Agnes and Kelty Outdoor Gear Industry

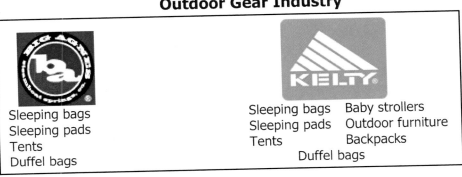

These four methods for defining a company's competitive scope can be used independently or in conjunction. Either way, the point is for business-level managers to make a conscious choice about the competitive scope. Instead of offering products and services to "anybody who will buy it," companies with a defined scope know what kinds of customers occupy their most critical market segments.

Competitive Advantage

In Chapter 3, the section describing the Resource-Based View of the firm established that a sustainable competitive advantage occurs when an organization's critical resources meet four criteria. The resources must be valuable, rare, hard to imitate, and exploited by the organization. These criteria provide a test for competitive advantage, but don't give guidance for crafting an overall strategy for the firm. According to Porter (1980) there are only two reliable foundations on which to base a competitive advantage: low cost or differentiation. If a firm chooses low cost, then all its resources should be acquired with the goal of building the lowest cost structure in the industry. Conversely, a differentiation strategy should mean that the firm is developing resources in a way that will create something unique for the customer.

The intent of a <u>low cost strategy</u> is to have the lowest cost structure the industry while providing goods or services that have competitive features and quality. Lost cost is an attribute of the organization's operations and efficiency – it is an internal characteristic that is under the company's control. It should not be confused with the company's *pricing* strategy, which should be related to cost but not wholly dependent on cost. When a company develops a cost leadership in the industry, it has pricing flexibility. It can set prices equal to the industry average and then earn above average margins. Or it can set prices below competitors' prices and have normal profit margins but higher market share. One implication of this definition is that studying a firm's prices is not a reliable method for trying to determine if it has a low cost strategy. It might have low prices but high costs because it is willing to accept low profit margins. In general terms, there are two methods that organizations can employ to achieve a

Figure 4.11: Methods for Cost Control

➢ Capture scale economies; avoid scale diseconomies
➢ Manage costs due to vendors & suppliers
➢ Consider linkages with other activities in value chain
➢ Find sharing opportunities with other business units
➢ Compare vertical integration vs. outsourcing
➢ Control percentage of capacity utilization

low cost advantage. First, the firm can perform its value chain activities more efficiently than competitors do. This method can be referred to simply as Cost Control. See Figure 4.11 for a list of specific options available to firms seeking to develop a low cost advantage.

These methods are not mutually exclusive – employing several will help the firm to become more cost competitive. Secondly, the firm can design its value chain to by-pass some typical activities. This approach can be called Cost Avoidance and is illustrated with several methods in Figure 4.12.

Figure 4.12: Methods for Cost Avoidance

➢ Simplify product design = fewer steps of production
➢ Find ways to bypass use of high-cost raw materials
➢ Use direct-to-end user sales/marketing approaches
➢ Relocate facilities closer to suppliers or customers
➢ Reengineer core business processes---be creative in finding ways to eliminate value chain activities

The theme of Cost Avoidance is to reduce costs by avoiding some common activities altogether. If one firm's value chain contains ten steps and its competitor's contains only six, the firm with the shorter value chain is likely to have a cost advantage. Making changes to avoid some typical costs usually requires some creative thinking. Most costs that companies incur seem to be necessary. Every year, costs increase incrementally and it seems impossible to delete any of them during a given budget cycle. Successful, innovative strategy always requires making hard and creative choices. Creativity can help with cost cutting innovations just as much as with customer service, marketing, and new product development. In the late 1980s Robert Crandall, CEO of American Airlines, launched a program called IdeAAs in Action. It was an internal program that gave all employees a financial incentive to use their creativity to uncover new ways to cut costs in the company. A flight attendant in first-class, Kathryn Kridel, noticed that the catering department received passenger information from the reservations department. It was a good idea because the catering department would load each flight with a sufficient amount of food to serve the number of passengers who had reservations for the flight. She noticed one problem, however. The minimum quantity of caviar was one can - 200 ounces – usually enough for about 13 passengers. On most flights, however, the first-class cabin had fewer than five passengers. Kridel recognized the waste that was created (especially since the caviar cost was about $250 per can). Using IdeAAs in Action she submitted a suggestion that the caviar should be purchased in cans of 100 ounces so there would be less waste. The final result was that her idea was implemented throughout the company. In 1992 her suggestion saved American Airlines $567,000 and she was awarded with a check for $50,000 (Robinson & Stern, 1998).

While a low cost strategy gives a company pricing flexibility and strong insulation against a price war, low cost isn't the best alternative for all situations. There are some conditions that make a low cost strategy especially effective. First, in situations where competition is for commodity products or products for which there is high standardization, a low cost strategy can be especially effective. When a market demands standardization instead of customization then it becomes easy for all providers to meet the standards. At that point, customers are likely to be especially sensitive to price differences because other features are similar in all the competitors' products.

The company that has the low cost structure will be best able to set low prices and still have positive profit margins. Second, when customers have low switching costs they are less likely to be brand loyal. They are usually willing to switch brands when there is a clear price advantage of one product over another. So when switching costs are low, the low cost provider can encourage switching behavior by low prices.

Conversely, there are situations when a low cost strategy is especially ineffective. These situations may be dictated by customers or competitors, but they also arise when companies have flawed execution of their low cost strategy. The first problem with low cost strategy is based on the concept of price elasticity of demand (see your microeconomics textbook for a review). The low cost leader in an industry might overestimate demand for the product when the price is lowered. If the price is lowered and there is not an increase in demand to offset the lower unit price then total revenue might fall instead of rise. The company will sell more units at the lower price but might not regain the lost revenue if the unit increase is small. Of course the increased unit volume might allow better economies of scale so the erosion in margins might be smaller than the change in price. The implication is that pricing strategy is complicated and *ceteris paribus*, lower prices do not always lead to stronger financial performance. Second, a low cost focus can become so pervasive that managers ignore other important aspects of the company's strategy. Some negative consequences can occur if the cost control mindset becomes too dominant: employees' salaries fall too far below the industry standards, the product or service provided has poor quality or high defects, the company gains a reputation as being "cheap," management ignores trends in its marketplace.

Pursuing a differentiation strategy requires a different set of competencies, resources, and tactics than a low cost strategy. As the name implies, differentiation requires the organization to create distinctiveness in its product or service that is both unique in the market and valued by some segment of the market. Notice a key distinction between low cost and differentiation: achieving low cost is an internal characteristic of the organization – there is a low cost leader in every industry, as measured by the relative cost structure of each competitor. But *differentiation is deemed successful by the market* – customers decide whether a company has achieved differentiation or not. Company managers might believe they have created a product that is valuable and unique but if the market doesn't share that view, then customers will not be willing to pay a price premium for the extra features that the product offers. As a consequence of differentiation being externally defined, organizations pursuing a differentiation strategy must be especially aware of "signaling," or how they signal value to their customers. Signaling is thought to be especially important in some situations. First, when the performance or quality of competing products is difficult to quantify, companies must be very intentional about educating the market about the value of their products. For instance, performance might be difficult to measure, so consumers choose a brand based on "gut instinct." A second, and related issue, is when customers are not experts in understanding performance differences between products. Maybe the performance differences can be measured accurately, but the measurement is too technical or esoteric for most consumers to understand. In the 1990s a famous advertising campaign was launched by Michelin. A whole series of TV and print ads ran for most of the decade and were widely recognized. See Figure 4.13 for an example.

All the ads featured an infant sitting in or near a Michelin tire. For most consumers, we are not sure how to compare one brand of tire against another. We know what size tire to buy, and we can compare prices. But evaluating characteristics like longevity, traction, fuel efficiency, and reliability are beyond our expertise. Michelin recognized this situation and decided to build its differentiation strategy around the concept of safety. The signal of value is clear and important: if you buy Michelin tires, you and your family will be safer on the roads. Instead of emphasizing the technical specifications of the tire, Michelin tried to differentiate its products by appealing to our sense of safety and security. A consumer might not believe that Michelin tires will provide better safety for his family but Michelin did become well-known for its advertisements. A third situation when signaling value is critical is when the product or service is purchased infrequently, which is probably also true of buying tires for a passenger car. When a product is purchased infrequently, consumers can lose track of the latest features and trends in the industry. So when it comes time to begin shopping a consumer will look for signals of value that is important to him or her.

There are probably dozens of ways that an organization can achieve a differentiation advantage. In important detail to remember is that differentiation can originate anywhere along the value chain, from beginning to end. Remember the example of Dell Computer Corp, from chapter 3. Dell's products are quite similar to its competitors but yet it became incredibly successful soon after its founding. The explanation is that Dell managed its inventory and relationships with vendors better than competitors.

Other companies are famous not for their products *per se*, but for their customer service, or convenience, or social responsibility, etc. In general, there are three common methods for achieving differentiation. See Figure 4.14 for a list.

Figure 4.14: Methods for Differentiation

➤ Lower the customer's overall cost of ownership
  • fuel efficiency
  • low maintenance costs
  • reduce complimentary costs
➤ Offer best performance on a key attribute of the product or service
  • highest durability
  • easiest to install
  • highest number of features
➤ Promote intangible or prestige features of the product or service
  • Associate the company with famous movie star or athlete
  • positioned for the elite / expert customer
  • available in limited supply or limited markets

First, a common method of differentiation is to lower the customer's overall cost of ownership compared to a competing product. Across its fleet of cars, Honda is known for fuel efficient engines. Honda creates value via the message that owning a Honda car will lower your gasoline costs because its cars provide high mileage per gallon of fuel. In chapter 3 the distribution system of Caterpillar Inc. was described as valuable resource that is very difficult for competitors to imitate. Caterpillar can deliver spare parts its customers to almost anywhere in the world faster than anyone in the industry. Instead of competing with Caterpillar's distribution system Komatsu tries to differentiate itself by durability, high quality, and consequently, low maintenance costs. Rather than shipping replacement parts quickly, Komatsu tells its customers that they will almost never need replacement parts because their equipment will not break down. If this promise to customers is kept, then customers can count on having low maintenance costs. Another approach to lower cost of ownership is to meet more needs of customers so your product or service allows them to avoid buying complimentary products. Many products meet two or more needs. One example is a combination leaf blower and vacuum or peanut butter and jelly combined together in the same jar. These products might not lower a customer's financial cost, but they add a convenience factor that can lower the overall cost (or burden) compared to buying both products.

Second, differentiation can occur by offering the best performance on one or more key attributes of the product or service. Casio's G-Shock watch is known as the most durable watch on the market. People who care about that feature are willing to pay a higher price for that performance. Titleist is widely considered as the golf ball that provides golfers with the best combination of feel and distance. In 2006, Titleist sold 43% of all the golf balls sold in golf course pro shops, according to Golf DataTech. That represents more market share than the combined sales of Calloway, Nike, Maxfli and Top-Flite. Transitions Optical, Inc. is known for manufacturing the best transition eyeglass lenses in the industry. These brands are known for being expensive, but to their loyal customers, the price premium is acceptable because they received added value compared to lower priced competitors' brands.

Third, differentiation can also be achieved by positioning a product as prestigious, fashionable, or desirable for intangible or non-economic reasons. In this type of differentiation, the functional performance of the product or service might be objectively better than its competitors. But not necessarily. Does a $400 Louis Vuitton purse perform better than an unbranded purse from Target? Does a Rolex watch keep time more accurately than a $40 Timex watch? The answer to these questions is "in the eye of the beholder." Companies that have successfully differentiated their products or services because of prestige have achieved success with a delicate mixture of marketing, design, research, pricing, and production.

In a given industry, there are dozens of possibilities for companies to compete successfully using a differentiation strategy. Circumstances that suggest a differentiation strategy can be effective occur when there is significant diversity of demand in the market, there are many competitors pursuing their own unique niche market, and when technological change is rapid. First, when customers are diverse and many varieties of needs exist in the market, it is usually difficult for one company to meet all those needs. Consequently, many companies emerge that specialize in meeting a subset of the demands in the market. Since a "one size fits all" approach is not effective for the market, customers find the provider that meets their specialized needs. In the retail banking industry, community banks have always been successful when they provide excellent customer service in a local neighborhood. Many customers want to know their banker on a first-name basis. Similarly, when competitors have diverged into serving different customer segments, there often remain unexploited pockets of demand that can be served by companies that grow into these segments. Third, fast-paced changes in technology mean that standards and expectations are always changing. As technological advances make more features possible (e.g. faster chips, smaller circuits, new compounds), customers want to participate in those changes by owning the latest and greatest version of a product. Technological change creates opportunities for companies that make discoveries in the research & development departments. For example, recent advances in the field of genetics have lead to new products in agriculture (genetically modified crops that are pest resistant) and medicine (genetic testing for disease propensity). Rapid technological change also presents opportunities for "disruptive innovations" (Christensen, 1990) that are often low-tech solutions that have been ignored by companies that continue to add more features to existing products. Sometimes a "good enough" product or service at a low price is exactly what some customers want. When products become too advanced, they inadvertently create opportunities for simpler products to fill the void. This problem is often called "feature creep," which occurs when "the engineers tend not to notice when more options make a product *less* usable. And marketing and sales departments see each additional feature as a new selling point, and a new way to lure customers. Often, the result is a product like Microsoft Word 2003, which has thirty-one toolbars and more than fifteen hundred commands" (Surowiecki, 2007).

As with a low cost strategy, there are common mistakes that should be avoided when pursuing a differentiation strategy. First, companies might fall into the trap of "feature creep" and add so many options to a product that it becomes unnecessarily complex. Too much differentiation makes a product or service too expensive and potentially frustrating for a consumer. A recent study by Philips Electronics "found that at least half of returned products have nothing wrong with them. Consumers just couldn't figure out how to use them" (Surowiecki, 2007). Second, instead of too much differentiation, some companies make the mistake of differentiating on the wrong attributes. For example, what features do you look for in the shampoo you buy? Everyone wants to have shampoo that cleans and protects their hair. We want it to smell nice and make our hair look good too. In the late 1970s, Clairol launched a shampoo product called "Touch of Yoghurt" (Haig, 2005).

Apparently there were not many people who wanted to associate washing their hair with the ingredients in yoghurt. Clairol added a feature to its shampoo that was not what people wanted. Sales were dismal and the product did not last long in the market. Third, charging an excessive price premium is a common mistake for differentiation strategy. Even if a company offers the proper amount of differentiation, aimed at the best features, the pricing must still be low enough that customers value what they are buying. We all expect to pay higher prices for higher quality but sometimes the price premium feels just a little too high.

Generic Strategy Matrix

In most cases, top managers must choose between broad or narrow scope and low cost or differentiation. As mentioned earlier, good strategy is about making wise trade-offs: successful companies rarely try to "be all things to all people." Instead, they determine their foundational resources and build a strategy to exploit them. Occasionally some companies claim they have a "best cost" strategy, which is a combination of differentiation and low cost. In all of these cases however, these are giant companies that began by pursuing either low cost or differentiation then pursued the other once they gained substantial market power. For most companies, choosing one or the other is usually wise. Otherwise the strategy is known as "stuck in the middle" – never taking a stand for any strategy and ending up on the border between the two. Competitive scope and competitive advantage can be arranged in a 2x2 matrix to illustrate the options for business-level strategy. See Figure 4.15.

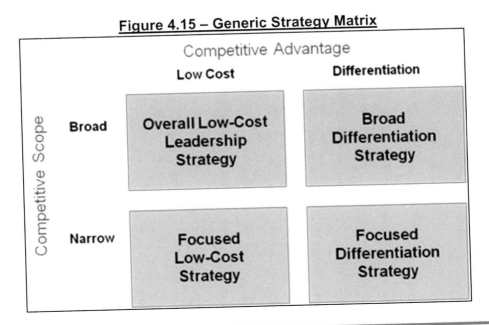

Figure 4.15 – Generic Strategy Matrix

Chapter 4: Corporate & Business Level Strategy

Based on the combination of competitive scope and competitive advantage, managers should be able to identify the cell that most closely characterizes their business-level strategy. Regardless of the industry, country, or economic situation, a company should choose one of these four strategies, then plan the details of the strategy using the Five Elements of Strategy (Figure 4.9). The generic strategy matrix creates four distinct strategies, one of which should be the obvious choice. The two strategies in the bottom row (narrow competitive scope) are sometimes known as "niche" strategies because they intentionally focus the company on serving a limited portion of the market. This brings us to the end of Step 3 in the Strategy Process Cycle (Fig 4.1). The verb motto for this step is "craft," indicating that creating strategy is partly a science and partly an art. Just as a sculptor crafts a piece of marble into a statue, leaders of organizations must know their own skills, know their environment and their audience, and be able to adjust to contingencies that occur during the process. Recall one of the definitions of strategy from Chapter 1 "strategy is a firm's theory about how to compete successfully." Building (or crafting) a theory amidst uncertainty is the highest calling of leaders today.

The third gate in the Strategy Process Cycle is "feasibility." This gate should remind leaders that strategy implementation (chapter 5) is considered the most difficult part of strategy. Any strategic plan should be vetted for its feasibility. Plans on paper always look great – but leaders must ask whether their organization has the financial, human, and physical competencies to execute the plan from paper into the real world of the organization.

For Further Consideration

This chapter describes business-level strategy as being a choice between **lost cost** and **differentiation**. Both can be achieved in a variety of ways. One famous example is the strategy of The Ritz-Carlton Hotel Company.

For five of six years Ritz-Carlton hotels scored the highest guest satisfaction ratings in the luxury hotel segment. See Figure 4.16 for the trend lines. The luxury segment serves the most demanding customers who have very high expectations. Two competitors (JW Marriott and Loews) have made huge increases in their scores over the past several years. Somehow, Ritz-Carlton has enjoyed increasing guest satisfaction and has managed to stay in 1st place. What is the strategy behind such outstanding performance?

Figure 4.16: Guest Satisfaction Ratings in Luxury Hotels
Source: JD Power & Associates

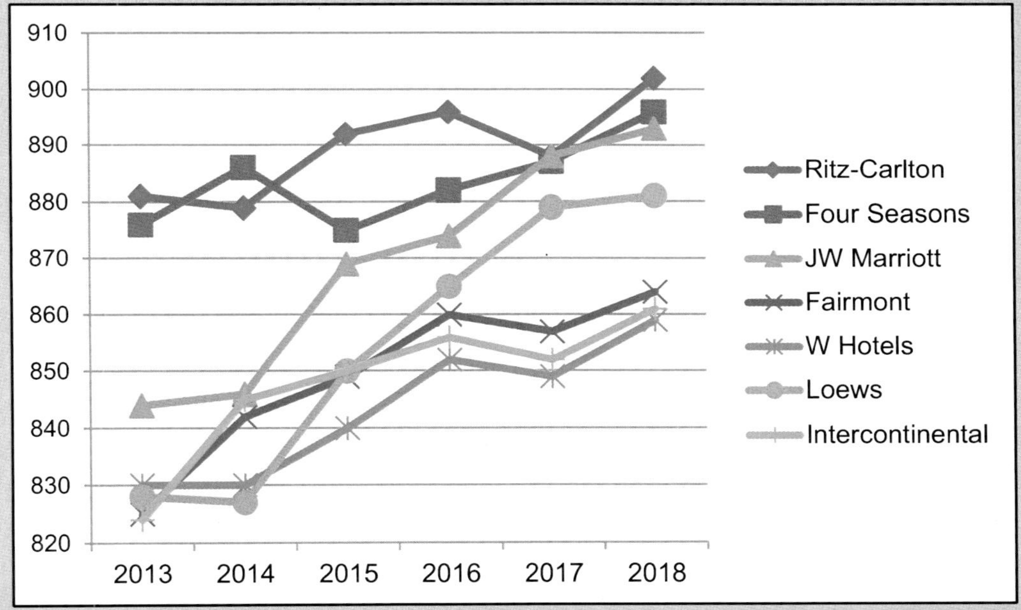

www.jdpower.com/business/press-releases/2018-north-america-hotel-guest-satisfaction-index-nagsi-study

Ritz-Carlton is a great illustration of interdependent activities forming a unified, high-performing strategy that has been difficult for competitors to imitate. The three activities are 1) choosing the best locations in the world for building hotels, 2) constructing the highest quality facilities in the industry, and 3) selecting, training, and re-training the best employees on the market. Every employee is authorized to spend up to $2000 when there is an opportunity to ensure that a guest has a remarkable experience at a Ritz-Carlton. The result is that employees across all departments are working toward the same vision – exceptional guest service. This is a great illustration of a differentiation strategy. Every employee is focused on excellent guest experiences without any exceptions. The result is that customers love the experience and are willing to pay outrageous prices to stay in a Ritz-Carlton.

Questions for Review & Discussion

1. Figure 4.3 in the text compares the differences between corporate and business-level strategy. In the left column are the common questions that must be addressed by an organization's strategy. Identify whether each question should be addressed at the corporate-level or business level of strategy.

Question	Business-level or Corporate-level strategy?
A. What competitive advantage do we have in this industry?	
B. How should resources be allocated across our portfolio of businesses?	
C. How do we gain market share?	
D. What synergy exists across our portfolio of businesses?	
E. In how many industries should we compete?	
F. What skills / resources need to be developed?	
G. What overseas markets are promising?	

2. The text discusses two main approaches for developing a Low Cost strategy. A list of actions is shown in the left column. Identify whether each action is part of the "cost control" approach or the "cost avoidance" approach. .

Action	Cost Control	Cost Avoidance
A. Capture scale economies		
B. Simplify product design		
C. Relocate facilities closer to suppliers		
D. Maintain high capacity utilization		
E. Share costs across several activities		
F. Avoid scale diseconomies		
G. Outsourcing		

Answers for Review & Discussion

1.

Question	Business-level or Corporate-level strategy?
A. What competitive advantage do we have in this industry?	Business level
B. How should resources be allocated across our portfolio of businesses?	Corporate level
C. How do we gain market share?	Business level
D. What synergy exists across our portfolio of businesses?	Corporate level
E. In how many industries should we compete?	Corporate level
F. What skills / resources need to be developed?	Business level
G. What overseas markets are promising?	Corporate level

2.

Action	Cost Control	Cost Avoidance
A. Capture scale economies	✓	
B. Simplify product design		✓
C. Relocate facilities closer to suppliers		✓
D. Maintain high capacity utilization	✓	
E. Share costs across several activities	✓	✓
F. Avoid scale diseconomies	✓	
G. Outsourcing		✓

References

Christensen, C. (1997). *The Innovator's Dilemma: When New Technologies Cause Great Firms to Fail*. Boston: Harvard Business School Press

Cyriac, J., Koller, T., & Thomsen, J. (2012). Testing the limits of diversification. *McKinsey Quarterly*, February, pp. 1-5.

Flint, J. & Mullin, B. (2019). AT&T takes on a Game of Thrones. *WSJ*. March 9, p. B1

Gryta, T. & Mann, T. (2018). GE Powered the American Century—Then It Burned Out. *Wall Street Journal*, Dec 14. https://www.wsj.com/articles/ge-powered-the-american-centurythen-it-burned-out-11544796010 Accessed 6/19/19.

Haig, M. (2005). *Brand Failures*. London: Kogan Page, Ltd.

Hoskinsson, R. and Hitt, M. (1994). *Downscoping: How to Tame the Diversified Firm*. Oxford: Oxford University Press.

Ilinitch, A. & Zeithaml, C. (1995). Operationalizing and testing Galbraith's center of gravity theory. *Strategic Management Journal*, 16:401-410

Klein, P. (2001). Were the acquisitive conglomerates inefficient? *RAND J. of Econ*, 32: 745-762.

Palich, L., Cardinal, L. & Miller, C. (2000). Curvilinearity in the diversification - performance linkage. *Strategic Management Journal*, 21: 155–174.

Porter, M.E. (1980). *Competitive Strategy: Techniques for Analyzing Industries and Competitors*. New York: The Free Press.

Reiss, R. (2009). How Ritz-Carlton stays at the top. *Forbes*. www.forbes.com/2009/10/30/simon-cooper-ritz-leadership-ceonetwork-hotels.html

Reppa, R. & Hirsch, E. (2007). The luxury touch. *Strategy & Business*. Spring, Issue #46. www.strategy-business.com/article/07103

Robinson, A. and Stern, S. (1998). *Corporate Creativity: How Innovation and Improvement Actually Happen*. San Francisco: Berrett-Koehler Publishers, Inc.

Sadler, P., Ryall, M., & Craig, J. (2003). *Strategic Management*, 2nd ed. London: Kogan Press.

Surowiecki, J. (2007). Feature Presentation. *The New Yorker*. May 28. Accessed on line at http://www.newyorker.com/talk/financial/2007/05/28/070528ta_talk_surowiecki

Chapter 5:
Strategy Implementation

Introduction

The fourth and final step in the Strategy Process Cycle is strategy implementation. The first three steps are mostly a mental exercise - planning, thinking and designing strategy. The last step (implementation) is how strategy is executed. After all the planning has concluded, employees in the organization must decide to carry out their roles according to the new or revised strategy. Do you remember the discussion in the Opening Vignette of chapter 1 on page 2? It described the message contained in this book's cover illustration. The previous version of the book used the game of chess to illustrate the concept of strategy, but the current version uses a picture of mountain climbers. Certainly the game of chess requires strategic thinking, but it doesn't require much complexity in implementation of a strategy. Typically, managers discover that planning and designing strategy (chapters 1-4) is easier than the implementation of the strategy (chapter 5). What makes implementation the most difficult aspect of strategic management?

First, implementing a strategy (especially a new strategy) involves **novelty**. The novelty might be in the form of a new strategy, new employees, new markets, new facilities, new products, or new competitors. Because effective strategy requires some innovation, implementing a strategy always creates some tension and uncertainty. Remember one of the definitions of strategy from Chapter 1: "strategy is a firm's *theory* about how to compete successfully." When it comes time to test the theory, managers know that mistakes are likely to occur because of the novelty of the implementation.

Second, successful implementation requires more teamwork and individual motivation than strategy formulation. In a nutshell, if employees don't "buy in" to the strategy because they disagree with it or because they are otherwise unmotivated to perform, then the strategy is unlikely to be successful. Consequently, good strategy implementation requires excellent "people skills," specifically skills in leadership and motivation. There are dozens of theories and hundreds of books on leadership. A full discussion of leadership is outside the scope of a strategic management course, but everyone should realize it is an essential part of effectively implementing strategy. For more information on leadership and motivation theories, study a good leadership book such as <u>A Leader's Legacy</u> by Kouzes and Posner (2006).

Third, strategy implementation is not guided by policies and procedures as clearly as strategy formulation. You might remember that Chapters 3 and 4 were full of techniques for assessing a company's situation. The techniques are described in a series of steps to be followed chronologically. As you will notice in this chapter, there is less concrete advice on the steps managers should follow for implementing a strategy.

Another introductory remark should preface the chapter on implementation. In virtually all strategic management models (including the Strategy Process Model in this book) strategy implementation is depicted as being *separate* from formulation, and of course occurring *after* formulation. In practice, however, good managers are constantly formulating plans, and testing to determine whether they are feasible while they are attempting implementation. The motto words in the Strategy Process Cycle (*dream, learn, craft, execute*) are not independent actions that are switched on, and then switched off. Instead, good managers are dreaming and learning constantly. They are always on the lookout for new ideas, opportunities, and trends that they can exploit. So, while strategic management models suggest that implementation always follows strategy formulation, the reality is that both actions occur in unison.

<u>Learning Objectives for Chapter 5</u>:
1. Distinguish the strengths and weaknesses of different organizational structures
2. Understand the role of corporate culture in strategy implementation.

Opening Vignette for Chapter 5

It's been a fantastic few years for Hilton Worldwide Holdings, Inc. A long-term turnaround strategy began after the Great Recession. The hotel company was bought and then sold by the Blackstone Group, the largest private equity company in the US. Then it went public in December 2013. In 2019, Fortune ranked Hilton as the #1 best company to work for in its annual list of Best Places to Work. Brand Finance identified Hilton as the most valuable hotel brand in the world, surpassing Marriott's brand by over $1 billion. The top 3 most valuable hotel brands are shown at the right.

While its brand was building equity, the stock market was rewarding Hilton. The graph below shows Hilton's stock market performance (ticker HLT in black) compared to the S&P 500 (purple) for the past 3 years. How did Hilton accomplish such an amazing turnaround in a slow-growth industry? According to CEO Christopher Nassetta, the main emphasis was on corporate culture and leadership. The secret was simple but powerful. Nassetta redesigned the culture around a unique version of hospitality: *treat every employee with the same level of hospitality as the guests receive*.

One of his first actions was to create an "immersion" program – not for new employees but for senior executives. All of them spent 2 weeks working as housekeepers, front desk clerks, and restaurant cooks. One of the executives complained that his housekeeping uniform was stiff, hot, and uncomfortable. So Hilton hired Under Armor to design and manufacture all new uniforms for the housekeeping staff.

Then, Nassetta rolled out programs to elevate the perks for all employees. In 2016, Hilton offered paid maternity leave to all employees, both salaried and hourly. Mothers who give birth get 10 weeks of paid maternity leave. "Go Hilton" allows employees to stay at Hilton properties at steeply discounted prices, and extends the offer to friends and family of employees. "Hilton HS Completion Program" helped its 5000 employees without a high school diploma get a GED.

The Hilton culture can be summarized as "identify the experience you need customers to have, and deliver the same experience to your employees" (Great Place to Work, 2019: 22).

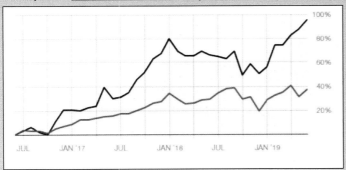

Nassetta strongly believed that if Hilton started treating its employees as fully part of the team, regardless of rank or role, then they would respond by providing excellent hospitality to the hotel guests.

Source:
https://tinyurl.com/y3xdl5vx

Organizational Structure

One of the most obvious realities of working in organizations is that employees have different job descriptions. Different people do different things. How are these responsibilities determined? Who decides which group of people will do one set of tasks as opposed to another set? Organizational structure identifies how work is divided into smaller tasks (differentiation) and how it is coordinated back together (integration). Without an organizational structure, companies would be inefficient at allocating labor to accomplish work. People would naturally gravitate to tasks that they enjoyed, but nobody would naturally choose the unpleasant jobs. The allocation of labor is important for efficiency, teamwork, and productivity in organizations. One of the earliest studies of organizational structure was conducted by Adam Smith, and reported in his famous book titled The Wealth of Nations (1776).

In one section of his book, Smith compared two different organizational structures for companies that manufactured straight pins. In one company, each employee performed all the steps in the process of making a straight pin. He would measure and cut a piece of wire, and then he would grind one end of the wire and attach the pinhead to that end. On the other end he would use a file to sharpen the wire into a point. The final step was to straighten the pin and pack it into a box. In today's terminology, we might call this a "batch" manufacturing process. In the other facility, employees were assigned to specific tasks in the process. For example, one person would measure and cut the wire, then pass it along to the next person who would attach the pinhead to one end, then pass it along to the person to grind the other end into a point. In both structures, the ultimate goal is the same: to produce straight pins effectively and efficiently. For a few moments, think about the outcomes that are important to the managers of these factories. First, consider the following: What should the managers measure? If managers were planning to pay bonuses to employees, on what criteria would the bonus be based? Second, based on those criteria, which organizational structure is better for manufacturing straight pins? Take a few moments to write down some answers to these questions. After spending a few minutes with these questions, see Table 5.1 for some additional insight into the comparison of the two structures.

Table 5.1: Comparing Organizational Structures

Criteria	"Batch" structure	"Sequential" structure
1. Productivity	Usually lower for a given time period	Usually higher productivity
2. Cost	Usually higher on a per unit basis	Usually lower because of higher output
3. Consistency	Usually lower	Usually higher
4. Job Satisfaction	Usually higher	Usually lower

The manager of a factory would probably try to encourage several measurable behaviors. He or she might pay a bonus for high levels of productivity (e.g. producing more than x number of pins during a day). Or, the manager might choose to encourage workers control costs by reducing scrap, reducing mistakes, and conserving company resources.

Table 5.1 compares the two structures using four different criteria. The first criterion, productivity, is usually easy to compare. Sequential systems usually are more efficient – the workers have all specialized in one or two areas and they become very proficient at them. Consequently they learn to complete their task quickly and as a team, are able to produce more pins that the same number of workers using a batch structure. Also, each worker uses only one tool, so he doesn't need to take time to change between tools.

Second, the cost of the two structures is related to the productivity. On a per unit basis, sequential generates a lower cost because it typically produces more output in a given amount of time (e.g. an 8-hour work day). Furthermore, employees in a batch structure may be able to negotiate for higher wages because they are cross-trained. They have multiple skills so might deserve better pay, compared to employees in a sequential structure.

Third, the consistency of the output of the two structures is usually higher in the sequential process. Due to task specialization, each employee in the sequential process repeats his task almost identically each time. In the batch process, each employee will probably make his pins consistently, but there are likely to be differences between the employees working in the batch system (e.g. a left-handed employees makes his pins a little differently than a right-handed employee).

The last criterion in Table 5.1, job satisfaction, might seem like an odd choice. Most managers don't measure it, and probably don't pay bonuses based on job satisfaction either. Adam Smith was not concerned with it when he wrote <u>Wealth of Nations</u>. Why might a modern manager care about job satisfaction as an outcome in his or her factory? Research has discovered that job satisfaction is an intermediate outcome that influences other outcomes. For example, if job satisfaction is really low, then productivity is also likely to be low. If people hate their jobs, they are usually not willing to exert effort to be productive workers. Similarly, when job satisfaction is low, both absenteeism (missing work for illegitimate reasons) and tardiness (arriving late to work) tend to increase. The lesson is that managers should be attentive to job satisfaction because it influences the outcomes that will influence the company's overall performance.

Figure 5.1 – The Influence of Organizational Structure

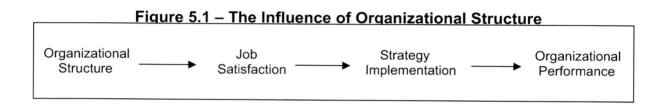

So, what's the point of referring to the study described by Adam Smith? It points to a chain of events that influences how an organization can become successful. See Figure 5.1 for an illustration. First, organizational structure influences job satisfaction. The way managers design jobs, tasks, and departments plays a role in how employees respond to their jobs. In the pin manufacturing plants, employees who were allowed to work on all stages of the pin, and eventually build an entire pin would have higher job satisfaction than those who completed only one step of the process all day long. Second, when employees are willing and able to do the tasks assigned to them, strategy will be implemented correctly. Third, when strategy is executed correctly, the whole organization's performance will improve. Figure 5.1 is a way to demonstrate that organizational structure does matter – it may seem boring and part of a meaningless bureaucracy, but it plays a crucial role in the strategic management process.

The importance of organizational structure was more recently illustrated when Microsoft Corporation announced a broad restructuring on July 11, 2013. According to the <u>Wall Street Journal</u>, the purpose was to "break down internal fiefs that have slowed product development and caused friction among teams of employees" (Clark & Ovide, 2013: B1). In its 37 year history,

Microsoft had become the most powerful software company in the world, but began losing its dominant position with the growth of Apple and Google. In recent years, Microsoft had been known for some successes like the Xbox video game console. However, the company's structure had been based around products, which resulted in some products being designed in isolation - independent from the work of engineers working on other products. For example, Windows 8 was launched as the new operating system that would work on both PCs and tablets. However, it "uses a different underlying architecture that prevents" it from working with Xbox and Windows smartphones (Clark & Ovide, 2013: B5). To ensure that future products will be designed with more collaboration, Microsoft CEO Steve Ballmer announced that the company will restructure "This means we will organize the company by function: Engineering (including supply chain and datacenters), Marketing, Business Development and Evangelism, Advanced Strategy and Research, Finance, HR, Legal, and COO" (Ballmer, 2013). The intent of the new structure is to help the company implement its new strategy of creating a family of devices and services for consumers and businesses. As its strategy shifts away from software and toward devices, Ballmer realized the company needed a new structure to implement its new strategy.

Types of Organizational Structure

Most organizations choose one of three basic varieties of organizational structure. The varieties presented below are generic versions – companies can certainly modify one of these designs to create a structure that fits their needs for implementation.

Functional Structure

A functional organizational structure is the most common of all types. It arranges people according to the function that they perform, such as accounting, marketing, finance, operations, HRM, MIS, etc. See Figure 5.2 for an example of an **organizational chart**, which is a graphical representation of an organization's structure.

Figure 5.2 - Functional Structure

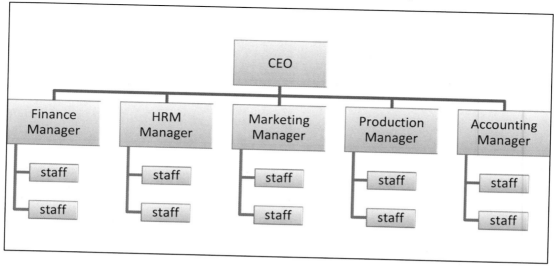

The advantages of a functional structure are that it allows better communication and coordination within the functional departments. Employees with the same background, training, and vocabulary are grouped together, so they are able to fully pursue their specializations. Conversely, the main disadvantage is that the organization can suffer from poor communication across departments. Some departments are notorious for having squabbles about making decisions in organizations. For instance, one stereotypical view is that accounting wants to reduce spending while marketing wants more money in its budget to attract more customers. Whenever goals between departments diverge, there is potential for conflicts to occur.

Divisional Structure

There are several forms of the divisional structure. Rather than grouping the departments by the function that they perform, all the versions of the divisional structure focus on an aspect of the market as their theme. The versions of a divisional structure are geographic, customer, and product structures.

Geographic structure is chosen when an organization's markets are widespread, and differences between the markets are great. Even if the distances between the markets are not great, it may be true that geographical differences create different product or service requirements. Geographical differences may occur due to weather, culture, laws, values, competition, or other factors. When managers notice that markets in one region are substantially different from other regions, it might indicate the need for a geographic structure. See Figure 5.3 for an illustration. The benefits of this structure are that each division can be designed to specially meet the unique needs of customers in its region. Sales, marketing, production, procurement, and all aspects of the value chain can be tailored to create the best product or service for the particular region. The main weakness of this structure is duplication of effort. Notice that in each division of Figure 5.3 the functional areas are repeated. So instead of having one finance manager for the company, each of the three divisions has its own finance manager. Of course some of these functions might stay at the corporate level, but many will need to be delegated into the divisions. A good example of a company structured according to its locations is Sykes Enterprises, Inc. According to its 2015 annual report "SYKES serves its clients through two geographic operating segments: the Americas (United States, Canada, Latin America, India and the Asia Pacific region) and EMEA (Europe, Middle East and Africa)."

Figure 5.3 – Division Structure (Geographic)

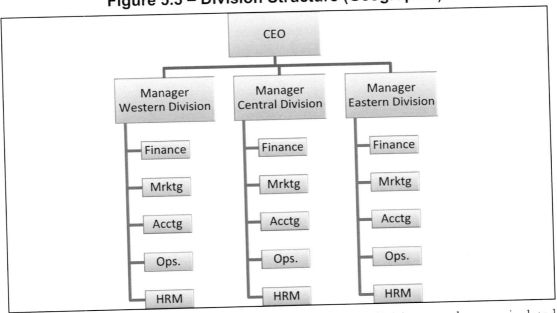

Another common weakness of the geographical structure is that divisions can become isolated from the other divisions and begin to act too autonomously. To make this structure work effectively, divisions must walk a fine balance. On one hand the division can act too independently while trying to serve the unique geographical market and fail to consider how it fits into the whole company. On the other hand it does need to create its own methods and systems for responding to the unique needs of the geographic region that it serves.

A *Customer Structure* is recommended when groups of customers can be identified that has such unique needs that they warrant service by a dedicated portion of the company. Figure 5.4 gives an example of a construction company that has three distinct groups of customers: Single Family Residential (builds single family homes for individual customers), Commercial (builds shopping centers, warehouses, and office buildings), and MultiFamily Residential (builds apartments and condominiums for developers). It could be the case that the each group of customers has very different demands, budgets, planning horizons, and need for customization. Working with a family to build their "dream home" is very different than building an office building for a real estate developer or a high rise apartment building. All are related because they are construction, but the end produce and the processes are different. In this case, it might make sense to design the organizational structure according to three divisions, each of which specializes on one customer group. The weakness of the customer structure is (again) duplication of the functional activities and potential isolation from the overall company goals.

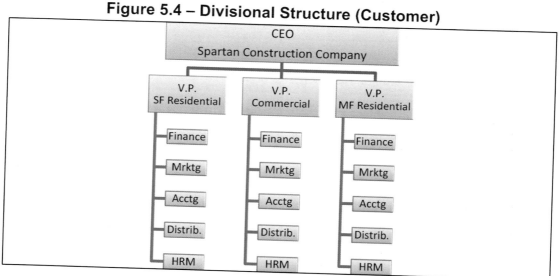

Figure 5.4 – Divisional Structure (Customer)

A *Product Structure* is illustrated in Figure 5.5. It is common in companies that have a corporate-level strategy (see chpt. 4) that includes diversification into more than one industry. Figure 5.5 illustrates the organizational chart of Bombardier, Inc. It's a large manufacturing company that builds two product lines for the transportation industry: small planes and trains. Because few (if any) of its customers buy products from both divisions, the divisions are free to build products to fit demands of their customers without concern for treading on the other division's market. While there is probably some potential synergy between the two divisions, the products are probably

Figure 5.5 – Divisional Structure (Product)
Bombardier, Inc

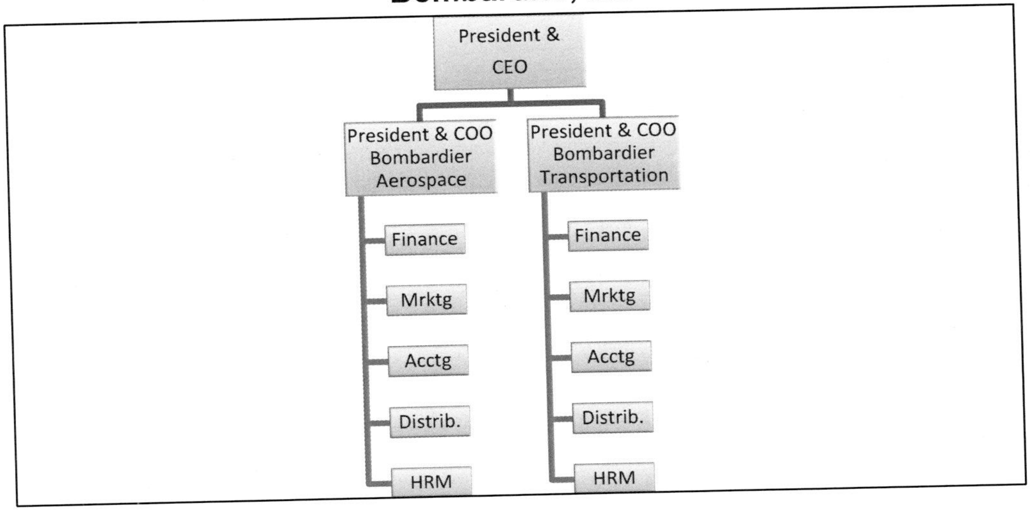

different enough that they warrant an organizational structure that allows them to work interpedently. This distinction is explained in the company's Annual Report:

> "These two manufacturing segments operate in the transportation industry, but they have different economic realities and face different risk profiles. The aerospace industry is capital intensive, with significant investment in product development and long recovery periods. The rail industry requires smaller initial investments which are usually recovered from specific contracts. The profitability of their respective operations reflects this reality" (Bombardier, Inc. 2008-09 Annual Report, p. 29).

In summary, a product structure allows a company to maximize its cross functional coordination within a product division. Every employee in the division, regardless of functional assignment, is working on the division's product. Just as with the other forms of divisional structures, the main weakness of product structure is that there is inherent duplication of effort across the divisions. Each functional area is repeated in each division.

Matrix Structure

The third basic type of organizational structures is known as a matrix. It is usually found in large multinational companies in complex industries. A matrix is a combination of a functional structure

Chapter 5: Strategy Implementation

and one of the divisional structures. In Figure 5.6, the matrix is a combination of a customer structure in the three columns and a functional structure in the four rows.

Figure 5.6 – Matrix Structure

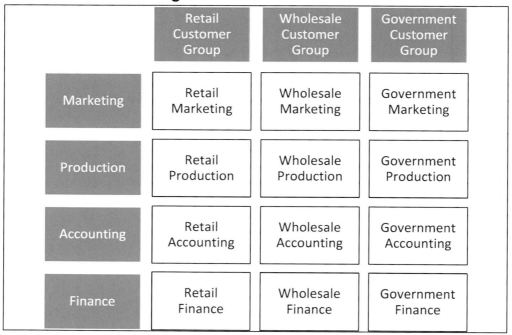

Each employee is assigned to a cell in the matrix, depending on his customer group and his functional expertise. The strength of using a matrix structure is that it keeps functional departments together (unlike the divisional structures) and helps coordinate interdependent business units or products. Coordination is expected to be strong because the matrix is designed to encourage information flows within the organization. Also, it is unlikely that any one division or perspective can become dominant because all the departments are interconnected. The main weaknesses are that a matrix is expensive and complicated to implement. Furthermore, it violates the idea that there should be a single "chain of command" for instructions and approvals to follow within an organization. For example if a person working in the "wholesale accounting" cell has a question, does he ask his accounting manager (horizontal) or his wholesale customer managers (vertical)? Or, what happens when his two managers give contradictory advice?

Whichever organizational structure is adopted within a company, managers should keep in mind that the sole purpose of structure is to help implement strategy. While there is no perfect structure, the structure should be designed so that it fits with the company's strategy. In fact, a common slogan adopted from research by Alfred Chandler (1962) is that "structure follows strategy," which means that a company's structure should be designed after the strategy is designed. Strategy is primary, and structure is secondary. Neilson, Estupiñán, and Sethi (2015:3) made a similar conclusion when they said "fix the structure last, not first." Many managers falsely believe that changing the structure will correct the company's problem. In almost all cases, a struggling company needs its leaders to create a better strategy, then design a structure to match.

Corporate Culture

The organization's structure is the *formal* approach to implementing strategy but corporate culture is an *informal* approach. Corporate culture can be a powerful influence on behavior and attitudes but it is not easy to document or transmit from one employee to another. It represents tacit knowledge while the organization's structure is part of its explicit knowledge. Corporate culture can be defined as the **values, beliefs, and norms that guide behavior and influence expectations within organizations**. These values, beliefs, and norms illustrate what is important to the organization and consequently they are passed down from senior employees to junior employees. One of the scholarly experts on corporate culture recently gave the following description of corporate culture.

> "Perhaps the most intriguing aspect of culture as a concept is that it points to phenomena that are below the surface, that are powerful in their impact but invisible…and unconscious. In that sense, culture is to a group what personality is to an individual. We can see the behavior that results, but often we cannot see the forces underneath that cause certain kinds of behaviors. Yet just as our personality and character guide and constrain our behavior, so does culture guide and constrain the behavior of members of a group through the shared norms that are held in that group" (Schein, 2004:8).

Attributes of Corporate Culture

There are two attributes of corporate culture that explain its impact on a company. First, the *intensity* of the culture is the extent to which employees understand and agree on the culture. So in organizations with a high intensity culture, employees share a clear understanding and commitment to the culture. There is strong unity that binds the employees together in their beliefs about what the company stands for. Conversely, in organizations with a low intensity culture there is substantial disagreement or misunderstanding about the company's culture. This situation usually occurs when there is weak leadership – nobody has clearly identified the vision and the purpose for the company.

Low intensity also occurs during transitional periods from one strategy to another, during a merger, downsizing, etc. During these periods employees are commonly unsure about the organization's culture because the immediate future is so unclear. Second, the ***integration*** of corporate culture is the degree to which business units or divisions have similar cultures. Especially in large organizations it is possible for one department to have a culture that is strong and intense, but different from the culture of another department. This lack of integration can occur across functions or across divisions, and within regions or across regions. To some extent, we would expect cultures to differ across departments. For example, the accounting department is likely to have a different culture than the marketing department, or the South American division of a multinational corporation (MNC) is likely to have a different culture than the East Asian division.

Purpose of Corporate Culture

What is the purpose or function of corporate culture? There are some people who assume that culture emerges haphazardly and without much intent from senior managers. Others, however, know that culture has a powerful effect on how effectively strategy is implemented.

First, culture ***conveys a sense of identity*** about the organization. Externally, the identity helps customers know what the company stands for and internally, culture indicates what its employees believe. Universally, customers want to trade with companies that are trustworthy. If a retailer gains the reputation as being untrustworthy it will certainly lose customers. Identity is important to employees because we all want to identify with the cause that our employer is pursuing. We want to believe that the organization is working to accomplish something greater than we can accomplish individually. Think about the example in the Opening Vignette about how Hilton worked with Under Armor to design lighter, more comfortable, and more attractive uniforms for all employees. As part of a team, an artistic performance, or a company, have you ever worn a uniform that was heavy, uncomfortable, or ugly? It probably didn't make you feel proud to wear it, and probably didn't help you perform better. Hilton CEO Christopher Nassetta wanted the employees to be proud to wear the Hilton logo on attractive, comfortable clothing. It's much easier to for employees to feel engaged at work when they are proud of their appearance and feel comfortable in their uniform.

Second, culture helps ***create a stable social system*** in the organization. During a week, full-time employees spend at least one-third of their lives at work. Friendships develop at work and employees can look forward to interacting with colleagues when the work is meaningful. Especially when work is difficult, people enjoy the friendships they develop during their employment. On the contrary, if employees report to work only to "earn a paycheck" then they are not likely to be highly committed to their colleagues or the company's mission. When a supportive, engaging culture exists in an organization, there are signs like bowling teams, company events, and strong teamwork.

Third, *culture guides behavior*. Many companies have an "employee handbook" or a "policies & procedures manual" that explain the formal rules and expectations of employees. The corporate culture is less formal but an equally powerful method of teaching employees what is expected of them in their daily interactions at work. Culture teaches people what's normal and expected. As new employees watch how veteran employees act, the new employees learn how to fit into their new roles.

These three functions of culture are generally positive. They are the intended outcomes that demonstrate why culture is an important part of strategy implementation. But there can also be some negative consequences of corporate culture. The most prevalent is that culture can so strongly define "how we do things here" that innovation and flexibility are suppressed. Industries and competitors change, but culture can create a barrier to change when it enforces norms with low tolerance for deviation. Specifically, a strong corporate culture can create barriers to diversity of thought and diversity of personnel. A strong culture can cause a group to reject something that is new and different (either a new idea or a new person) because it does not fit the "normal" profile in the company. Xerox provided a famous example of a culture that discouraged a major innovation. In the early 1970s researchers PARC, a subsidiary of Xerox, invented the first PC, laser printer, LAN, and mouse. They were using the computers, networking them together, and developing software to run them. In spite of the internal success of these innovations at PARC, Xerox was never able to commercialize them. According to one reviewer "PARC scientists quickly developed a reputation for brilliance matched only by a reputation for bad manners. An alumnus of the center admits, 'PARC suffered from a whole lot of arrogance. If you didn't understand automatically, you were `stupid.' It's hard to get a good hearing that way.' An irreversible case of communications gridlock set in between PARC and the rest of the corporation" (Graulich, 1989).

Communicating Corporate Culture

At the beginning of this section, corporate culture was described as being passed down from senior employees to junior employees. In most organizations, there are several channels through which the knowledge of culture is learned.

1. Stories and myths – Tales of past success, expert employees, victories against competitors, etc. are ways that new employees learn the history of their employer. Within each story, of course, is a moral or a lesson that demonstrates the correct or appropriate action that new employees should adopt. While many stories are about historical events, stories can also be told about current (or recent) events. If a noteworthy event occurs one day, managers can use the event the next day to demonstrate cultural norms for both senior and junior employees. Nike has recently concentrated on telling meaningful stories to share the values that leaders believe are important. "Nike has made understanding its heritage an intrinsic part of its corporate culture. Think of this approach as internal branding: The stories that you tell about your past shape your future. Which is why, these days, Nike has a number of senior executives who spend much of their time serving as 'corporate storytellers' -- explaining the company's heritage to everyone from vice presidents and sales reps to the hourly workers who run the cash registers at Nike's stores (Ransdell, 2007).

2. Rituals and routines are actions that symbolize an important value or belief. In themselves, they don't really mean anything. But the actions point to or highlight something that should be cherished and remembered. An American tradition is to eat turkey on Thanksgiving Day. What is special about turkey on that day? It is available in the grocery stores all year long, but most of us eat it only one day per year. The turkey symbolizes the meals that the early US colonists had with the indigenous people – the dinner that the pilgrims had with the Indians. We cherish the freedom that America has gained because of those early settlements. Companies can also have rituals that are meaningful reminders. John Sculley, former VP in PepsiCo described a ritual at the company "Like other meetings, this one was a ceremonial event. We marked it on our calendars many weeks in advance. Everyone wore the unofficial corporate uniform: a blue pin-striped suit, white shirt, and a sincere red tie. None of us would ever remove the jacket. We dressed and acted as if we were at a meeting of the board of directors" (Sculley & , 1988:2). This ceremonial meeting reinforced the culture of PepsiCo that required order, respect for authority, dedication, and deadly serious competition against Coca-Cola.

3. Norms and values are signals of "how we should act" or "what we believe is good and true" in organizations. Norms are anything that the organization considers "normal" behavior. In some organization, always accepting the ideas of your boss is normal, but in other organizations the bosses expect employees to question their authority and make alternative

suggestions to their ideas. In many Japanese companies, each employee is expected to stay at work until his boss has left for the day. The norm is that you should work at least as many hours as your boss works. This example applies to Japanese culture more than the corporate culture of a particular company, but it still illustrates how norms influence behavior. Many companies have explicitly stated values that are non-negotiable. The values at Levi-Strauss & Company are described as "We are a company guided by our values: empathy, originality, integrity and courage, and with them in mind, we constantly strive to build a culture just as inspiring as the people who wear our clothes" (Levi-Strauss website).

4. Reward systems are the most formal means by which corporate culture is managed and communicated. If well-managed, the reward system in an organization will encourage desired behaviors and discourage undesirable behavior. Stated more eloquently, the reward system "defines the relationship between the organization and the individual member by specifying the terms of exchange: it specifies the contributions expected from members and expresses values and norms to which those in the organization must conform, as well as the response individuals can expect to receive as a result of their performance. The reward system—who gets rewarded and why—is an unequivocal statement of the corporation's values and beliefs. As such, the reward system is the key to understanding culture" (Kerr & Slocum, 2005:130). Most managers realize that the most effective compensation is a mixture of base pay plus performance-based pay. When the performance-based pay rewards the desired behavior, employees will understand what actions will result in higher compensation. Related to the reward system is the formal training and "onboarding" that new employees experience when they join an organization. Here, they are taught rules and regulations that reflect the organization's culture.

Figure 5.7 - The Strategy Process Cycle

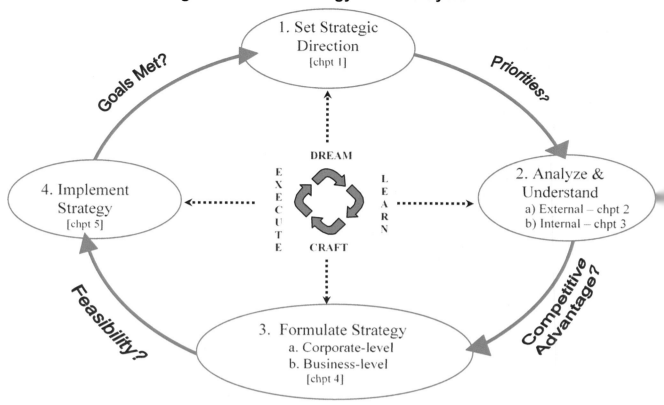

The conclusion of this chapter brings us to the end of the Strategy Process Cycle (Figure 5.7). The gateway question at the end of step 4 is "goals met?" As strategy is implemented, managers must compare actual results to goals as a means of determining whether the strategy is having the intended effect. If goals are not being met, managers need to determine if 1) the goals were set too high or 2) if the goals were appropriate but were not met. In that case, managers should try to determine why the goals were not met in preparation for beginning the Strategy Process Cycle again.

Closing Remarks

Now, at the end of this short book, you should have a better idea about "How Strategy Works." The Strategy Process Cycle is a model that can be used to guide strategic thinking, but it is only a model (i.e. a "simplification of reality"). It reflects modern research and best practices for how strategy should happen. Remember: strategy is both a noun and a verb! Strategy is a thing – how we will get our organization into a successful future – but it also must be a continual activity of evaluation and renewal. To conclude the book, there are three assumptions about successful strategy that don't fit neatly into any single chapter. These are the KSFs (see Chapter 4!) that must underlie any leader's approach to developing strategy.

❶ Good strategy requires good people skills: this assumption seems obvious, but it was never stated explicitly in the book until now. For a leader to accomplish *every single stage* of the Strategy Process Cycle, he or she must be effective at working with and leading other people. "Developing strategies is ultimately a people-centric process fueled by conversations" (McKinsey Quarterly, 2014:9). Of course a thorough study of leadership is outside the scope of this small book, but the importance of leadership skills cannot be over-emphasized in any discussion about strategy. Changing and improving an organization's strategy always requires some employees (maybe all employees) to change their behavior. As we know, old habits die hard. Changing behavior is hard for all of us but effective leaders excel in encouraging people to change. The first step in making a change is to envision a different and attractive future....remember the first step of the Strategy Process Cycle is setting the organization's mission and vision.

❷ Good strategy requires good questions: this assumption shows that strategy always requires people to collect information. There are many kinds of information that might be collected. For example, we might collect information that is irrelevant, or obsolete, or inaccurate, or incomplete, or fleeting, or contradictory. Furthermore, we must collect information that describes many things. For example, a strategist must know about competitors, industry trends, laws, colleagues, bosses, and of course, himself. All this means that a good strategist will know how to ask good questions. *Strategy is a critical thinking exercise*, which demands good questioning. This book contains many strategic thinking frameworks, but the frameworks are not strategy and they don't create strategy for you. The frameworks are designed to guide your thinking – so that you can apply your own creativity and instincts to them. Don't ever let frameworks, models, or questions replace strategy.

❸ Good strategy requires trade-offs: because every organization faces scarcity of resources, strategists must *learn to say "no."* Even a wealthy organization cannot pursue every opportunity, so good strategists will choose to deploy an organization's scarce resources toward the best goals. Another common way to convey this idea is with the phrase "good is the enemy of great." In other words, it might be a mistake to pursue many good things at the expense of pursuing a few great things.

For Further Consideration

In this chapter, the concepts of organizational structure and corporate culture were covered in separate sections. In practice, however, they are interdependent characteristics of every organization because both are informed by the company's fundamental values. Take the example of Zappos, the on-line shoe retailer. Above all, Tony Hsieh (founder and CEO of Zappos) cares about whether people are happy. "I've been trying to come up with a unified theory for happiness," he says (Chafkin, 2009). This might sound like an unusual hobby for the CEO of a billion dollar company. But for Hsieh, happiness is not just a hobby; it is the value that drives the decisions for his whole company. "What he really cares about is making Zappos's employees and customers feel really, really good" (Chafkin, 2009). His over-arching value of happiness is reflected in the structure and culture of Zappos.

In the company's structure, call center operators have incredible amounts of freedom and autonomy. "Unlike most call center operators, Zappos does not keep track of call times or require operators to read from scripts. One of them, Grace Hale, has a penchant for offering unsolicited commentary on customers' shoe selections – 'They are beautiful,' she coos during one call, as she pulls up a picture of a pair of Dr. Scholl's Asana heels that a customer found uncomfortable. Not only are reps encouraged to make decisions on their own -- for instance, offering a refund on a defective item -- they are supposed to send a dozen or so personal notes to customers every day."

Culture is so important to Zappos that even prospective employees are exposed to it. "Customer service reps start at $11 an hour, warehouse workers at $8.25. But even in its hiring process, Zappos creates wildly different expectations than do most companies. Prospective hires must pass an hour-long 'culture interview' before being handed off to whatever department they are applying to. Questions include, 'On a scale of 1 -- 10, how weird are you?' and 'What was your last position called? Was that an appropriate title?'"

Sources:
Chafkin, M. (2009). The Zappos way of managing. Inc. May.
http://www.inc.com/magazine/20090501/the-zappos-way-of-managing.html

Parr, S. (2012). Culture eats strategy for lunch. Fast Company, Jan. 24.
http://www.fastcompany.com/1810674/culture-eats-strategy-lunch

Questions for Review & Discussion

1. According to the text, the importance of designing the best organizational structure can be illustrated in a four-step process. Arrange the steps into the correct sequence.

    - Job Satisfaction
    - Organizational structure
    - Organizational performance
    - Strategy Implementation

2. According to the text, there are several generic forms of organizational structures. Examine each figure below and identify which structure it illustrates.

A) This figure illustrates a _____ structure

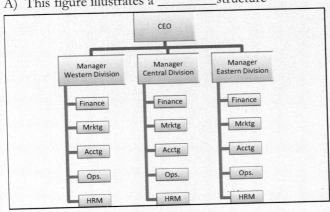

B) This figure illustrates a _____ structure.

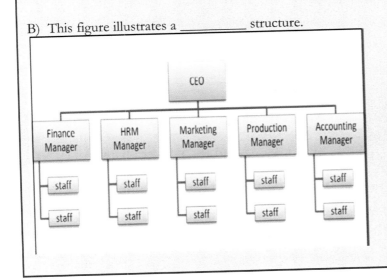

Answers for Review & Discussion

1. See Figure 5.1 for an illustration

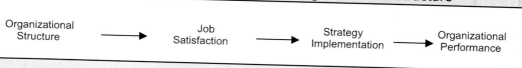

Figure 5.1: The Influence of Organizational Structure

Organizational Structure → Job Satisfaction → Strategy Implementation → Organizational Performance

2. Figure A is a Geographic Structure (See Figure 5.3 for a review)
Figure B is a Functional Structure (See Figure 5.2 for a review)

References

Ballmer, S. (2013). Internal communication to Microsoft employees. Available at http://www.microsoft.com/en-us/news/Press/2013/Jul13/07-11OneMicrosoft.aspx

Clark, D. & Ovide, S. (2013). Ballmer solidifies grip on Microsoft. *The Wall Street Journal*, July 11, p. B1.

Graulich, D. (1989). "Fumbling the Future: How Xerox Invented, Then Ignored, the First Personal Computer. - book reviews". *Washington Monthly*. Accessed 19 Aug, 2009. http://findarticles.com/p/articles/mi_m1316/is_n5_v21/ai_7675535/

Kerr, J. & Slocum, J. (2005). Managing corporate culture through reward systems. *Academy of Management Executive*, 19: 130-138.

Levi-Strauss website https://www.levistrauss.com/2017/05/09/us-best-employer/. Accessed 7/13/19

McKinsey Quarterly (2014). What strategists need: a meeting of the minds. September: 1-14.

Neilson, G., Estupiñán, J., & Sethi, B. (2015). 10 principles of organizational design. *Strategy &*: 79:1-6

Ransdell, E. (2007). The Nike Story? Just Tell It! *Fast Company*, Dec. 19. Accessed on line at http://www.fastcompany.com/magazine/31/nike.html

Schein, E. (2004). *Organizational Culture and Leadership*, 3rd ed. San Francisco: Jossey-Bass.

Sculley, J. & Byrne, J. (1988). *Odyssey: Pepsi to Apple... a Journey of Adventure, Ideas and the Future.* New York: Harper & Row.

Smith, A. (1776). *The Wealth of Nations*. London: W. Strahan and T. Cadell.

Index of Topics & Companies

About the Author

George H. (Jody) Tompson is a professor of management and entrepreneurship at The University of Tampa. He has also been on the faculty of the University of Waikato (Hamilton, New Zealand) and the University of Central Arkansas. He earned his PhD in strategic management from the University of South Carolina in 1995. His undergraduate degree is from Trinity University (San Antonio, TX) where he earned a BS in finance and a BA in English in 1987.

He is also the Director of the Naimoli Institute for Business Strategy at The University of Tampa. The Institute runs an innovative program that matches local companies with student teams for the purpose of building strategy. See www.ut.edu/naimoli for more information.

In 2010, Jody founded CitriClean of Florida, LLC. It is a company that manufactures an all-natural consumer product designed to make automatic dishwashers work better. Many US states banned phosphate from detergent in 2009, and CitriClean was created to solve the problem of "cloudy dishes" that often occur in regions where hard water is prevalent. See www.CloudyDishes.com

Jody is married to Dr. Holly Tompson, PCC, who is the Director of Coaching Services at LandIt, Inc. She has also been the Associate Director of Coaching in the Doerr Institute for New Leaders at Rice University, a professor of management at Florida Southern College where she taught MBA courses in leadership and international business. They have three children and reside in Tampa, FL.

Made in the USA
Columbia, SC
07 July 2022